Shame has plagued us from the beginning, but in God's redemptive story, it has no final word. With humor, authenticity, and biblical wisdom, Aubrey Sampson writes to proclaim good news: in Jesus, we have a Savior and a Shame Remover.

—JEN POLLOCK MICHEL, author, *Teach Us to Want*

Scripture couldn't be clearer: "There is *no condemnation* for those who are in Christ Jesus." Yet we continue to hide behind the wall of shame. Aubrey Sampson calls us out from our hiding place and into the freedom that is already ours. With honest storytelling and practical application, she nudges us forward and then beautifully kicks our backsides to step boldly into who we already are in Christ.

—ELISA MORGAN, speaker, author,
The Beauty of Broken and *Hello, Beauty Full*

For any woman who has experienced insecurity or shame, Aubrey Sampson's words offer truth, joy, and healing for the soul. Filled with humor, biblical insight, and no apologies, Aubrey offers women hope instead of despair, grace instead of grief, and beauty instead of ashes. Read *Overcomer* and rebuild your identity as a woman free from shame.

—GEORGIA SHAFFER, author, *Avoiding the Twelve
Relationship Mistakes Women Make*

Shame is far too powerful in most of our lives. *Overcomer* is not a miracle cure, but it's the next best thing. Prepare to reclaim your past and discover your fullest self!

—LESLIE LEYLAND FIELDS, author, *Forgiving
Our Mothers and Fathers*

This winsome and practical book will resonate with so many women, both for its stories of shame and its roadmap for finding the way out. Let it lead you toward freedom.

—AMY SIMPSON, author, *Anxious: Choosing
Faith in a World of Worry*

Shame is toxic to our faith. Through the pages of this book, Aubrey Sampson will take you on a journey to discover its devastating nature. Aubrey presents bold truth to help usher you into deeper intimacy with Christ and empower you to overcome shame. As a pastor, I am excited to recommend this book because I know it will be a great tool to introduce many people to the fierce love of God that brings true freedom!

—KENNETH E. ORTIZ, *Redefined: Discovering and
Celebrating What God Really Thinks about You*

With wit balanced by insight and honest confession, Aubrey helps us face the pain of shame with hope and truth. For all those ashamed to deal with shame, let Aubrey hold your hand to the cross.

—MITCHEL LEE, pastor, Grace Community Church

I work with thousands of women and never has there been a more urgent message in our quest for wholeness in Christ than uprooting the lies about shame. *Overcomer* is relatable, practical, and purposeful in sharing the steps to inner freedom. A perfect small-group study.

—PAM KANALY, author, speaker, cofounder of Arise Ministries

Aubrey tenderly walks you through the hidden hurts and fears we all carry and hide. Through Scripture and story, she winsomely invites you in to real and powerful times of healing and restoration.

—CINDY JOHNSON, author, *Who's Picking Me Up from the Airport? and Other Questions Single Girls Ask*

Aubrey Sampson is well-acquainted with shame and what it takes to overcome it. In this book, you'll find great help and encouragement to kick down the walls of shame as you learn to think rightly about God, yourself, and the world.

—MARLENA GRAVES, author, *A Beautiful Disaster: Finding Hope in the Midst of Brokenness*

Are you drowning in overwhelming public shame or silently hounded by unwanted thoughts of regret or self-loathing? *Overcomer* reveals a tender Jesus with the power to transform our stories of shame into identities soaked in love. A resource every woman needs. With honest stories, accessible tools, and worksheets, *Overcomer* provides what you need to rebuild your soul.

—SHAYNE MOORE, author, founder of Redbud Writers Guild

In my years of ministry to women, I've learned that, for so many, you don't have to scratch too far beneath the surface to encounter some form of shame. This book provides a dynamic, solid, biblically based toolbox for those who are ready to be set free from shame's crippling effects in a loving, practical, and powerful way.

—TERRI KRAUS, president, Redbud Writers Guild; author of The Project Restoration series

OVERCOMER

Aubrey Sampson

OVERCOMER

*Breaking Down the Walls of Shame
and Rebuilding Your Soul*

ZONDERVAN

Overcomer
Copyright © 2015 by Aubrey Sampson

This title is also available as a Zondervan ebook. Visit www.zondervan.com/ebooks.

Requests for information should be addressed to:

Zondervan, 3900 *Sparks Dr. SE, Grand Rapids, Michigan 49546*

ISBN: 978-0-310-34258-8 (softcover)

ISBN: 978-0-310-34261-8 (ebook)

Published in association with literary agent Heidi Mitchell of D.C. Jacobson & Associates LLC, an Author Management Company, *www.dcjacobson.com*

Cover design: Dual Identity
Cover photography: © ronfromyork / Shutterstock® / © nicolecioe / iStockphoto®
Interior design: Denise Froehlich

First printing August 2015 / Printed in the United States of America

This book is dedicated to *The Sundays*.

Your picture was next to my computer the whole time I wrote, and in so many ways, this book was designed for and inspired by you. You have blessed me.

May you always live without shame.

Her vacant eyes above forced smile reveal
how worn she is from all she, silent, knows.
How beautiful she'll be when her lips peal,
the chains fall, she speaks out, she blossoms, grows.
And so a megaphone for the defiled
Will rise up from the fragile billboard child.

—LYDIA BUSH, "BILLBOARD SIGN"

Lift your face, Love; Raise your eyes, Child.
Beauty streams from you.
Shame was vanquished—Hope is shining;
God can get you through.

—LYDIA BUSH, "AFTER ALL"

I sought the LORD, and he answered me;
he delivered me from all my fears.
Those who look to him are radiant;
their faces are never covered with shame.

—KING DAVID, PSALM 34:4–5

CONTENTS

FOREWORD

Grabbing the cleaning supplies, a roll of paper towels, and the For Sale sign, we headed into the woods toward the clearing that had been home to our gently used RV for the past decade. Now that our kids were older, it was time to retire from camping and pass the RV on to another family. We had agreed on an asking price of only $1,000, indicating our generosity and our desperation to have one less item to maintain. A couple of hours of scrubbing and polishing and she'd be good as new and ready to roll.

But when we opened the door, unexpected sights and smells greeted us. Rather than the layer of dust we'd anticipated, a layer of mold decorated the wood cabinetry, and mildew adorned the upholstery, curtains, and carpet. The sagging, water-stained ceiling told the sad story of a neglected recreational vehicle whose roof had sprung a leak in the eight months since it had last been used.

"Let's roll out the awning and see if there are any salvageable parts," Greg suggested. My husband, always the optimist. But as we maneuvered the awning brackets loose, the entire frame fell at our feet with a *thud!* My mental stability crashed to the ground with it.

"I can't do this!" I screamed like a banshee and bolted toward our log cabin, leaving my husband standing there stunned. I hurled myself onto the first bed I encountered, gut-wrenching sobs escaping from somewhere deep in my soul. Within thirty seconds, the internal dialogue began.

Oh good grief, Shannon, what's all this? You were ready to get rid of the RV anyway! Now you don't have to clean it—just torch it! It's not like we desperately needed the money.

And you can't be mad at Greg—the RV is as much your responsibility as it is his, and neither of you had any idea about the leak! Come on—what is all of this REALLY about?

At the time, we were reading a book called *How We Love*. Authors Milan and Kay Yerkovich describe these bewildering emotional outbursts as "triggers"—when the soul's response far outweighs the circumstances. They suggest asking the questions, "What am I really feeling, and do I remember feeling this way as a child?"

That didn't take a lot of pondering. I was feeling overwhelming shame—a feeling that became a close companion at the age of ten. That year, my parents fulfilled their dream of moving to the country, and that was when my nightmare began.

We'd lived in a cute little neighborhood with white picket fences and honeysuckle vines, pecan trees for climbing and backyard storm-cellar clubhouses where friends gathered until sundown. The day the movers arrived, they didn't bring cardboard boxes and a moving van. They brought two flatbed trucks and crowbars to pry off the underpinning. Our house was split in half and then covered in plastic. I watched it roll down the road, unaware that such a thing was even possible.

I didn't know we lived in a mobile home. It had been so well disguised by our concrete porch, flower beds, and holly bushes. In its new location, ten miles from downtown Greenville, Texas, there would be no white picket fences, no honeysuckle vines or holly bushes. Only a hayfield that would soon become home to my mechanical-genius father's projects—ancient cars, rusty air-conditioning units, and moldy refrigerators that would have benefited more from burying than repairing.

I'm not sure why, but the underpinning didn't go back on for quite some time, nor was a new concrete porch poured immediately. We climbed in and out our front door on makeshift steps of rickety wood pallets adorned by a lime green carpet remnant. Classy.

This new living arrangement might not have been so bad had it not been for the fact that I had to ride the bus to school every day and the bus picked me up directly in front of my house. The wheels underneath our home seemed to proudly proclaim the "poor white trashiness" of it all. And every time I boarded that bus, I saw my fellow passengers' eyes—looking at me, looking at my mobile home, surveying the surrounding junkyard, and looking back at me with a smirk that clearly stated, "At least I'm better than you."

The emotional pain of boarding that bus every day for six years was eclipsed one day by physical pain. I was fifteen and counting down the days until my sixteenth birthday and my first car, which would surely rescue me from those daily condescending stares. After chatting too long with a friend after class, I realized I had missed the bus home. Part of me was relieved I didn't have to ride it. The other part was in a panic. I had no idea how I'd get home. That's when I saw Richard Jenkins emptying his locker. As a senior, surely Richard had his own car. I nonchalantly approached, batted my Maybe-It's-Maybelline eyelashes, and begged him to give me a ride, digging into my Jordache jean pockets to see how much gas money I could produce as a bribe.

My plan worked. We left the school parking lot and I gave him turn-by-turn directions, leading him out into "the sticks" where I lived. But with two more turns to go, it suddenly dawned on me that Richard was about to see where I lived. I couldn't do it. I just couldn't bear guiding him into the driveway that made me cringe. So I told him to keep driving down the highway until he came to a beautiful red brick house with a towering oak tree in front and a sprawling barn in back. Robin Morrison's house. She wouldn't be home yet, so surely no one would know about my shameless scheme to avoid even more shame.

The only problem was that Robin lived more than two miles away from my mobile home. Richard dropped me off, and there I was—in bright blue high heels, carrying a ten-pound backpack full of books. I walked two miles in those shoes, which took me well over an hour and kept me in flats for more than two weeks while the bloody blisters healed.

As an adult, I've actually become grateful for my modest upbringing and the strong ethics my hardworking parents instilled in me. When I hear Miranda Lambert sing "The House That Built Me," I think of my parents' house, where they still live today and have labored diligently over the past thirty-five years to "enhance its ambiance."

But the residual shame still rears its ugly head sometimes, as it so clearly had on this RV-cleaning day. After wisely giving me a few minutes to decompress, my husband gingerly entered the room, inquiring, "Honey, what just happened out there?" I explained the childhood memories that had come flooding back with tsunami force. Greg responded exactly the way Milan and Kay Yerkovich recommended—with compassion and concern. He scooped me up in his arms, tucked my head into the crook of his neck, and began rocking me back and forth. "Shhhhh," he insisted. "It's okay. You never have to be embarrassed about where you live—not ever again." Yes, I melted into his arms, and I can shamelessly proclaim that this turned into one of the sweetest lovemaking experiences we'd ever had. (I'm known as "the Sex Lady," so surely you expected a sex scene somewhere in my story, right?)

Over the past twenty years of ministry to women who've looked for love in all the wrong places, I've learned that if we look beyond the fruit of their actions, we so often discover a root of shame. Since the Every Woman's Battle series began releasing in 2003, emails have flooded my inbox from women who've been used, abused, taunted, or tortured. Some have turned not just to relationships with men (or women) but also to alcohol, drugs, cutting, binging, and so on. Others medicate with more socially acceptable actions such as obsessive dieting and exercise, workaholism, or perfectionism. It's amazing what unresolved emotional pain and shame can drive humans to do—incredibly destructive things that usually create added layers of shame. It can be a vicious cycle.

But sometimes shame simply stays buried deep in the psyche, and people manage to disguise it quite well. Perhaps you're one of those people who can fool everyone, projecting the image that you've got it all together. Perhaps you're even one of those people who have disguised your shame so well that even you don't recognize it.

I'm so glad Aubrey has chosen to bring her wisdom and experience to helping women identify and overcome the vicious cycle of shame. I was thrilled when she applied to participate in my twelve-month online mentorship program called BLAST (Building Leaders, Authors, Speakers, and Teachers). And when we later met face to face, I felt an immediate connection, like I'd encountered the "cool little sister" I never had.

Over the coming months, I was impressed by the progress Aubrey made as an effective communicator. When she asked for additional coaching in developing a book proposal, I was honored to come alongside her. But I had no idea what God was about to do—both in Aubrey and through Aubrey. As she wrote, she healed. As she healed, she blossomed. And as she blossomed, she gave her readers (including me) the courage to heal from their own shame and to blossom as well. This process was a vivid reminder of how writing and simply sharing one's story with others can sometimes be the most effective therapy available.

I knew God would open doors for Aubrey's message because it is so clear that this is not just her message. It's God's message, which he's lovingly entrusted to her faithful stewardship—a transformational message for you, and for me, and for all who've walked in this shame-filled world.

Just as Jesus redeemed the shame of a Samaritan woman at a well, an intimate disciple who'd denied him three times, and a crowd who mocked and scorned and crucified him, Jesus stands ready to redeem the shame in your story as well. As you turn these pages, may you feel God's loving embrace envelop you tightly, rock you gently, and heal you completely.

—*Shannon Ethridge, bestselling author and advocate for healthy sexuality*

Dear Fabulous Reader,

The "quotables" opening each chapter (see next page) were designed with you in mind. I invite you to take photos of your faves and pin, post, share, tweet (or do whatever social media verb you're into) with #overcomer. In this way, you'll be interacting with and helping to spread the word about *Overcomer*, while also encouraging your friends and followers to find the freedom from shame that is theirs in Jesus.

As always, live shamelessly,

Aubrey

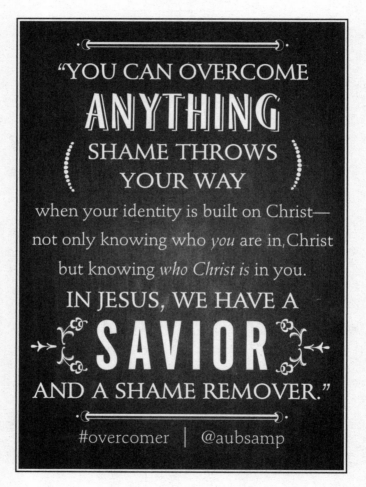

"YOU CAN OVERCOME **ANYTHING** (SHAME THROWS YOUR WAY) when your identity is built on Christ— not only knowing who *you* are in, Christ but knowing *who Christ is* in you. IN JESUS, WE HAVE A **SAVIOR** AND A SHAME REMOVER."

#overcomer | @aubsamp

Chapter 1
LET THE DEMOLITION BEGIN

Dismantling the House That Shame Built

I was uberfabulous in middle school. That is to say I had purple and pink braces and my bangs were teased up to the clouds. I had a jean jacket with shoulder pads, a jean purse, and a jean skirt. So yeah, I was pretty awesome. But in the eighth grade, I developed an unfortunate condition that redirected the course of my entire middle school career. I came down with D-cups.

Eighth grade was also the year I discovered my first love. Several times. I was obsessed with Dylan McKay, the rebel character of the TV show *Beverly Hills 90210*; Alex Pawlak, my basketball-playing boyfriend; and two ninth-grade boys named Hoppy and Bo (yes, really), who rode my school bus.

My school district bused a few unlucky freshmen along with the middle schoolers, and they hated riding with us "little kids." But to me, these older students were gods. The boys had facial hair. The girls wore miniskirts. They chewed tobacco and talked about their parents' divorces. They were *90210* made flesh. The day Hoppy and Bo invited me to sit with them in the back of the bus, I knew my life was about to change forever. Me! An eighth grader! Invited to sit in the back of the bus with the cool kids.

They included me in their inside jokes, showed me how to tie a cherry stem with my tongue, and (because this was Oklahoma) taught me the art of dipping. On my first and last attempt, I stuffed the fat wad of tobacco into my lower lip and waited to experience whatever thrill I was supposed to feel.

After about thirty seconds, I threw up all over the floor of the bus.

I was humiliated, mortified, certain my new status of cool was forever covered in puke. All of my fears quickly evaporated when Bo put his arm around my shoulder to comfort me. "I'm sorry, cutie. I should have known you couldn't handle it."

Oh, the power of that sound, the siren call of that sweet nothing, "cutie." *These high school boys think I'm a cutie.* My entire sense of self, my total identity, had changed. Suddenly, I was no longer Aubrey, the awkward eighth grader. I was Cutie, the object of affection. For what felt like the very first time, I was noticed by someone other than my parents. I was somebody. I mattered.

I sat with Bo and Hoppy on those worn-out avocado bus seats, enraptured. High on their attention, intoxicated by their flirtations, I idled away time fantasizing about Hoppy inviting me to the high school dance, or daydreaming that Bo would ask me out on a date.

A few months into the school year, Bo finally popped a question: "Hey cutie, have you ever played Fire Drill?"

I tried to come up with a cool answer to hide the fact that this was categorically not the question I had been hoping for, but before I could form a coherent response, Bo was yelling, "One, two . . ."

Wait? Are we playing now? Aren't you supposed to run around the outside of the bus or something? I barely had time to register what was happening. On "three," Bo lifted my arms over my head, shoved me flat on the bus seat, and hissed, "Hurry! We're close to her stop!" After taking a quick look to make sure no one could see him, Hoppy lifted up my shirt and groped my D-cups.

When I think back on that day, I can still remember some details. I can vaguely recall the stinging sensation at the back of my head because a strand of hair was caught in one of those stubborn metal window latches. I remember praying the other kids on the bus wouldn't turn around and see what was happening; I was afraid they'd make fun of me. I noticed Bo's acne scars for the first time and wondered how I'd never seen them before. Honestly, though, I wasn't aware of much, except for one overpowering emotion. A feeling, at the time, I would not have been able to name. Now I know—I felt shame. I was ashamed because of what was happening, but there was another shame, deeper and more toxic. I was humiliated because it was happening while I was wearing a white training bra. I didn't want Hoppy and Bo to think of me as an inexperienced, unsophisticated little girl. I was ashamed of myself.

When the bus lurched to a stop in front of my house, the boys released me. I readjusted my clothes and blundered off the bus steps, shaken and confused. I could still feel the calluses of Hoppy's hands against my skin and hear Bo's taunt ringing in my ear: "I like your little white bra, cutie. You better not tell anyone about this, *cutie.*"

My favorite nickname reduced to a jeer.

I stood in front of my house, my mom playing inside with my little sister, and wondered what to do. I could run inside and tell her everything. She'd hug me and cry, probably call my dad. My parents would have sought justice. The police would have been involved or the school, or Hoppy's and Bo's parents. I never would have had to ride the bus again.

But I was scared what the boys would think. I was nervous they'd tell their friends. I didn't want to be uncool. I didn't want to uncutie. Frankly, I wasn't entirely sure that it wasn't my fault—that it wasn't my body's fault for developing those breasts so early.

The thirteen-year-old in me didn't have the vocabulary to describe what had happened. The Office on Violence against Women defines sexual assault as any type of sexual contact or behavior that occurs without the explicit consent of the recipient.[1] But I didn't know the term sexual assault even existed. If I did, I'm not certain I would have given myself permission to use such a strong word. Assault would have felt too big, too powerful, too important somehow. It would have made me seem like the victim of something. I wasn't sure I wanted to be a victim. I wasn't even convinced I *was* a victim. I liked them, after all. I vied for their attention. Did I invite this?

When evil entered the world, God asked Adam and Eve what happened. Adam's response was simple: "The woman made me do it." At thirteen, without any hesitation, I believed the oldest lie in the book: what happened was my fault because I was female. I never told a soul.

As a grown woman and mother to three sons, I want to shake those ninth-grade boys and say, "What were you thinking? Who taught you that was okay? You better not lay a finger on any other girl!" I want to yell at the bus driver, "Where were you? Why weren't you paying attention?"

Mostly, I want to grab the hand of that scared little girl standing in the driveway and lead her into the house. I want to wrap my arms around her and say, "Let's go tell Mom. She'll take care of this. Daddy'll know what to do."

I want to look her in the eyes, stroke her cheeks, and say, "Hey, precious girl. It's okay. There's nothing to be afraid of. You are made in the image of God, and this was not your fault. You do not need to be ashamed."

I want to attend to her, cry with her, and assure her that keeping silent will be worse than the momentary discomfort of telling. More than anything, I want to protect her from what will happen in the months and years to come.

What Is Shame?

Shame encompasses such a wide range of emotions it can be difficult to define. Perhaps the simplest way to understand it is to think back on a moment when you experienced it. You may have felt embarrassment, discomfort, or self-consciousness. Shame can also express itself in much weightier emotions, such as when we feel humiliated, inadequate, or injured.

Another difficulty with shame is that so many women live under the weight of it without knowing it because they've been conditioned by culture and life experience to accept that feeling as normal. Shame is simply always there. It's that familiar yet profound feeling that we don't measure up. Dr. Brené Brown, a leading expert on shame in women, describes it this way: "People often want to believe that shame is reserved for the unfortunate few who have survived terrible traumas, but this is not true. Shame is something we all experience. And while it feels like shame hides in our darkest corners, it actually tends to lurk in all the familiar places, including appearance and body image, motherhood, family, parenting, money and work, mental and physical health, addiction, sex, aging, and religion."[2]

While it's certainly not the only emotional issue we deal with, like my friend Lonn Obee says, shame is similar to the phenomenon of learning about a new car you've never heard of before and then suddenly seeing it everywhere. (That's the Baader-Meinhof phenomenon, for you trivia people. You can now show off at parties.) Once you begin to recognize shame, you realize how much it permeates your life.

Think about it. Maybe you regularly view life through the lens of other people's expectations (real or imagined) and you're beginning to buckle under the pressure. Maybe you're ashamed of how you look. You want to control your changing body, so you obsessively count calories or exercise compulsively, and you're weary from the effort. Maybe you regularly criticize yourself. You feel the need to be all things—smart, sexy, and successful—but you are tired of striving (and failing) to measure up to some elusive standard of womanhood. Perhaps you feel self-conscious about not having a boyfriend or a happy marriage when all of your friends seem to be content in their relationships. Perhaps a friend stabbed you in the back, one of your parents was emotionally or physically absent, or your loved one has a secret addiction, and you think it's all somehow your fault. Shame is lurking in all of these things.

You could be stressed about your children and how you are handling things at home. The voice in your head says, *I'm not a very good mother.* Maybe you feel like a failure because life got hard and now your dreams are out of reach, or you just don't know who you are anymore. Perhaps you've experienced so much loss and grief that you can't help but think *you're* the problem. Maybe you go through life with ever-present feelings of inadequacy; you worry what other people would think if they knew the real you. Possibly you've been fighting a life-long battle of some kind, and it seems like anyone else in your shoes would handle it better than you. Shame is hard at work in your struggles.

And there's the pressure we get in our Christian culture to operate above reproach *all the time*, which leads us to feel ashamed when we make even a tiny mistake. We may be-lieve that if we *aren't* shaming ourselves, we're in danger of becoming prideful. So we beat ourselves up as the "better," more Christlike option. It's a vicious cycle. With family, cul-ture, society, and even our faith community's expectations of what and who we should be, shame can be overwhelming as well as confusing. (I could go on and on, but at this point, I'm just depressing us.)

My first conscious experience of shame was birthed during, and grew to fruition soon after, the bus incident. The follow-ing weekend, a group of girlfriends and I went to hang out at the mall. While my friends were busy flirting with boys at the food court, I slipped away to go shopping at a lingerie store. If something like the bus incident were ever to happen again, I was determined not to be caught in some little girl's under-wear. I prepared for the worst, covering one of my first experi-ences of shame with the defensive wall of sexiness.

The root of the word shame is actually derived from the phrase "to cover."[3] Adam and Eve were so ashamed of their sin they covered themselves with fig leaves. Shame became their new wardrobe, and it became mine. I spent the rest of the school year riding at the front of the bus, never looking back, but always feeling Hoppy's and Bo's eyes on me.

The Shame Identity

In his book *Healing the Shame That Binds You*, John Bradshaw writes, "To have shame as an identity is to believe that one's being is flawed, that one is defective as a human being. Once shame is transformed into an identity, it becomes toxic and dehumanizing."[4]

At its core, an identity of shame is the belief that, *in whole or in part, I am not enough*. Because shame has so many nuances and can trigger a wide range of emotional reactions, I've come to think of the shame identity as a house of lies made up of seven rooms. (See figure.)

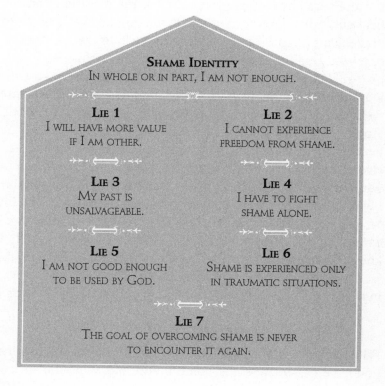

SHAME IDENTITY
IN WHOLE OR IN PART, I AM NOT ENOUGH.

LIE 1
I WILL HAVE MORE VALUE
IF I AM OTHER.

LIE 2
I CANNOT EXPERIENCE
FREEDOM FROM SHAME.

LIE 3
MY PAST IS
UNSALVAGEABLE.

LIE 4
I HAVE TO FIGHT
SHAME ALONE.

LIE 5
I AM NOT GOOD ENOUGH
TO BE USED BY GOD.

LIE 6
SHAME IS EXPERIENCED ONLY
IN TRAUMATIC SITUATIONS.

LIE 7
THE GOAL OF OVERCOMING SHAME IS NEVER
TO ENCOUNTER IT AGAIN.

As it did with Eve's first bite of apple, something twisted awakened in me after that bus ride, and I began to take up residence in a Shame Identity of my own. On the one hand, I was still a normal teenager: I had fun with my best friends; I performed well in school; I enjoyed my family; I was generally happy. But an inner emotional shift had taken place, and at such a young age, I was unable to name it or protect myself from it. As I look back now, I liken that shift to the difference between holding a cherished photograph of a loved one and being with that person in the flesh. Photographs capture emotion, evoking a smile, a laugh, a poignant memory. But nothing can compare to the sensory experience of hearing a loved one's voice, wrapping your arms around them, inhaling their scent, and seeing their laugh lines. Photographs are beautiful, but they are always only facsimiles of the real thing. Shame held out its hand to me that day on the bus, and I allowed it to drag me into a darkroom and develop me into the 2-D version of myself—still smiling, but a replica of the original.

You'd think an experience like that would have me screaming and running as far away from men as possible. As time went on, it had the opposite effect. I discovered that my body attracted attention, and I became needy for more. Over the next few years, I had one unhealthy relationship after another, always attempting to fill a growing emptiness, to prop up a withering self-esteem. I needed a man's attention or I felt like I was invisible. I struggled with body image and was so intent on gaining approval from the opposite sex that I forgot how to express myself. Without a boyfriend "educating" me, I didn't know what music or movies I enjoyed, what books I should read, what clothes I liked to wear. I didn't know my own voice. In every sense of the word, I shrank. (Including those D-cups.)

Deconstruction

While you may not relate to every detail of my story, I imagine you have known, at some point in your life, what it is to feel unworthy or disqualified, what it means to feel like that 2-D version of yourself. You've probably shed secret tears behind locked doors. You may have painful memories or emotions of your own. You may have allowed yourself to disappear a little bit. I'm willing to bet the little girl inside needs to learn how to believe she can overcome her shame.

In construction work, there are multiple ways to demolish a house—detonation, wrecking ball, even bulldozing. But there is also a gentler demolition technique known as deconstruction, in which a house is carefully dismantled in order to reclaim and repurpose the valuable and beautiful elements. Throughout this book, we'll carefully break down the walls of shame and dismantle all seven lies one chapter at a time, but not with a wrecking ball. Instead, we will gently deconstruct the shame from your life, all the while preserving the valuable and beautiful elements in order to rebuild your soul—in order to allow you to begin taking up space in your life again.

My prayer is that through the pages of this book, you will be built up and equipped with all the tools you need for restoration: a practical theology for overcoming shame, biblical truths, next steps, discussion questions, prayers, a little laughter along the way, and inspiration from personal stories written by brave women who've overcome shame in their own lives. Returning to my story, I'll share some of the more painful experiences from my life, along with some of the more absurd ones. *(Hi. My name is Aubrey. I'm a woman who inadvertently causes scenes in public.)* Together, we'll raze the shame so we can raise the roof on a new identity that's free from it.

The Overcoming Shame Identity

A few years ago, to my chagrin, my husband, Kevin, brought home a colossal artificial Christmas tree. Towering well over two stories tall and lit with brash blinking lights, the thing is gaudy enough to have its own act in Vegas. Needless to say, monstrous trees are not meant for small houses. Each December, while other families create holiday spirit by traveling to farms to chop down quaint little postcard trees, we stay inside sweating our faces off. We squeeze furniture into tight corners, jam decorative items anywhere they'll fit, haul fake tree limbs up and down the stairs. We do whatever it takes to create enough space in our living room for "The Giant."

If it weren't for our three boys, the effort would definitely not be worth it, but they adore the thing. It serves as their secret clubhouse—a place to stash cozy blankets and stuffed animals, a nook for snuggling up with hot chocolate and Christmas books. On some nights, they'll even camp out underneath the tree, and I love watching their chubby cheeks flash red, blue, and green under the twinkling lights. This enormous object, which shouldn't otherwise fit in our home, has become a cherished centerpiece of our family's memories and traditions.

To be an overcomer is to allow the expansive love of Christ to take up so much space in your life that shame no longer has any room to grow. If the Shame Identity is a house made up of seven lies, then the Overcoming Shame Identity is a house built on truth. In place of the sign that says, "In whole or in part, I am not enough," it has a banner hanging over it that reads, "In Jesus, I can overcome." It is a house whose foundation is beautifully described by the psalmist: "Those who look to him are radiant; their faces are never covered with shame" (Ps. 34:5).

The Hebrew word for radiant, *nahàr*, is sometimes translated "to beam with joy." It's a beautiful contrast to the dark covering of shame. The promise of Scripture is that when we look to Jesus, our shame is transformed into sparkling, beaming joy, with more dazzle than any giant Christmas tree. There will still be moments in life when we feel condemned into little more than a pile of ashes, a heaping mess of secret insecurities. But when our identity is centered in Jesus, we can discard the dark covering of shame and rise in radiance. That's a promise—one I can make from personal experience.

Jesus took our sin on his shoulders, forever changing our eternities, but he also did something else. He took our shame to the cross. Jesus endured the cross and *scorned*—looked down on, despised, had no respect for—its shame (Heb. 12:2). How cool is that? Jesus *shamed* shame! And in doing so, he transformed the *in whole or in part I am not enough* identity. See the truth is, in our sinfulness we aren't enough. But the gospel shatters our shame identity because we are declared enough through Christ, who is more than enough. Through his death and resurrection, he offered himself to us and for us, and demolished the power of shame—forever.

If you find it hard to believe this for yourself right now, that's okay. Freedom from shame is a journey that happens one step, one hope, one healing at a time. For now, I invite you to hold on to a truth I believe strongly enough for the both of us: you can overcome anything shame throws your way when your identity is built on Christ, not only knowing who *you* are in Christ but knowing *who Christ is* in you. In Jesus, we have a Savior and a Shame Remover. We have a sovereign Ruler who compels our shame to bow down before his authority. We can overcome shame because our Overcomer already has.

Even if your past is dark, even if you've spent your entire life feeling like a replica of yourself, even if you think you don't measure up, even if you've been hiding in shame for years, in Jesus, you are no longer the not-enough girl. You are no longer the girl on the bus. You are no longer the girl crying behind locked doors.

You are that girl rescued.

That girl rebuilt.

That girl renewed.

That girl the overcomer.

DISCUSSION QUESTIONS

1. In what ways might your life be different if you could be free of shame? For example, consider the impact on your relationships, aspirations, confidence, and faith.

2. Think back over the last few days. What kinds of things—small or large—triggered shame in you? Which of the seven lies comes closest to describing how these experiences influence your identity?

3. If you could talk to a younger version of yourself, what might you say about shame? How would you reassure her of God's love?

4. What, if anything, makes it difficult for you to open your heart to those same reassurances now?

5. If you could name one goal—an aspect of your inner life you'd like God to transform while you read this book—what would it be?

PRAYER

God, I praise you because even in my darkest moments you were there. While I don't fully understand it, I know you have the power to help me overcome shame, because you've already done so on the cross. Open my heart to experience your love and mercy, and forgive me when I allow shame to keep me focused on myself. Help me receive whatever it is you want to teach me. In the name that is able to remove my shame, the name of Jesus, amen.

CATHERINE
Overcoming Childhood Shame

I think of the early years of my childhood as the garden of Eden, full of nurture and love and beauty. But just like the first family in the garden, when a member of my family made a tragic mistake, we were all banished forever. And I do mean this literally.

My childhood ended the day we were told we had two weeks to leave the only community I had ever known—my entire world. Few friends were willing to walk this road alongside my family, but shame readily came along with us. It was not the original sin, so to speak, that introduced me to shame, but the rejection that followed. It is a harsh reality for a child to suddenly discover that the world is a place in which you can be exiled because of a mistake you or someone else made. And it was even worse to discover that my family and I were apparently worthy of such abandonment.

Two varieties of shame became my constant companions. The first came when I was with someone who didn't know my story. This shame sat by my ear and said, *Never, ever trust.*

Never, ever let someone know you. There was always something to hide, a desperate need to keep acquaintances and potential friends at an arm's length lest they discover that we were not to be accepted, not to belong, not to be loved in spite of weakness. This shame was my closest friend for over a decade—from age twelve to my early twenties. During that time, I never once spoke about what had happened. No one knew the secret that made me who I was and accounted for so many of my thoughts and feelings.

The second variety of shame came in those rare instances when I was around people who knew—family or friends who lived in or near the community we had left. This shame sat near my other ear and said, *Never, ever ask the questions you are wondering; never, ever speak of this out loud.* So questions such as, "Do you still love us?" and, "What do you think of what happened?" and, "Are we safe with you?" were never voiced, and never, ever answered.

Shame is powerful because it tells us we are slaves. Like anyone exerting wrongful power, shame hides the truth of freedom in fearful threats, telling us we can never be free because we can never show our faces to anyone without shame. But the freeing truth is the opposite—we can be seen, we can be known, we can be loved, and better still, we can be *redeemed.*

I have been exiled, but I have also been redeemed. We cannot always keep shame from walking in the front door, but we can crowd it out—with friendship, truth, forgiveness, and the love of Christ. I experienced this for the first time at age nineteen when I finally mustered the courage to tell the truth to a few friends. They loved me then, and they love me still. Now, in place of shame, I have memories of restoration and healing. I remember the night I stayed up with my family, talking, crying, praying, forgiving. I remember the very moment I confronted the hate in my heart and chose forgiveness instead. I remember the many miracles—some seen with my eyes, some felt in my heart—that helped me take baby steps on this journey away from shame. It has been a long, hard journey, especially in those early healing years, but through it all, Christ, and not shame, is the victor.

Redemption brings beauty from ashes. Without the breaking, I could not have been healed; without the exile, I could not have been redeemed. And realizing these truths is a redemption in itself.

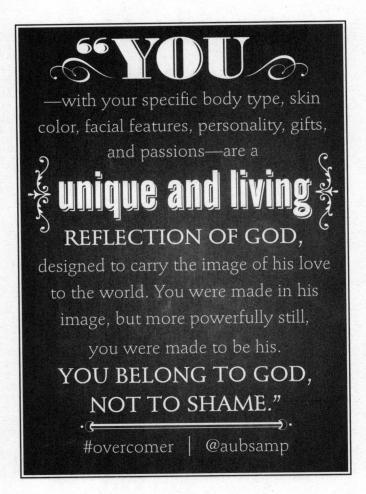

"**YOU**
—with your specific body type, skin color, facial features, personality, gifts, and passions—are a

unique and living

REFLECTION OF GOD, designed to carry the image of his love to the world. You were made in his image, but more powerfully still, you were made to be his. YOU BELONG TO GOD, NOT TO SHAME."

#overcomer | @aubsamp

Chapter 2

CRACKS IN THE FOUNDATION

*When the Pressure to Have It All
and Balance It All, While Looking Like the
End-All, Is Turning You into a Hot Mess*

SHAME'S LIE: I WILL HAVE MORE
VALUE IF I AM *OTHER*.

OVERCOMER'S TRUTH: I AM CREATED IN
GOD'S IMAGE WITH EXCEEDING WORTH.

I am about to confess something to you. Get ready because this is a huge, nay, a paradigm-shifting revelation. Are you ready? Okay, here goes nothing. I'm a reality television and celebrity gossip junkie. I'd like to tell you I just casually watch "E! News" when I'm flipping through channels or that I happened to stumble upon it once or twice. But that'd be a big fat lie. If it's on E! or Bravo, it has at one time or another been on my DVR list.

I don't have much spare time to watch television these days, but if I'm folding laundry or jogging at the gym, these shows are my favorite distraction. I've even read some of the Real Housewives' books. If I ran into one of the Housewives at the local grocery store (not that women this famous ever set foot into grocery stores; I'm almost certain they import their food items from someplace grand and mysterious like Bhutan), I'd probably knock you over for her autograph. I'm *that* person. #fangirl.

As much as I love my guilty pleasure, I'm intelligent enough to know this cultural phenomenon is missing a dose of reality. I mean, I don't know about you, but I don't have paparazzi stalking me at the aforementioned grocery store, which is probably a good thing. With the birth of my third son came the death of my ability to dress myself like a normal human adult. As actress and writer Mindy Kaling says, "There has ceased to be a difference between my awake clothes and my sleep clothes."[5] (If a Housewife's bodyguard saw *this* coming toward his client, he might be sorely tempted to reach for his taser gun.)

We can't talk about shame without discussing the cultural frenzy that fosters it. Just a few years ago, if you were in a grocery store aisle or at the doctor's office and you stumbled upon a magazine cover featuring an extraordinarily thin (and obviously airbrushed) waif of a woman, you could silently protest by simply turning the magazine over. But now? From our phones, to our devices, to our television sets, to the latest E! news report about whichever media princess lost her baby weight at warp speed, the world's beauty-image communique is everywhere. In *So Long, Insecurity*, Beth Moore describes the new normal of media-driven comparisons like this: "Most of our great-great-grandmothers had access to compare themselves to a few hundred women in a lifetime. We can now throw ourselves up against tens of thousands if we're willing— and apparently most of us are. We've got travel, television, the internet, magazines, books, billboards, movies, storefronts, advertisements (even on the back of the cab in front of us and the bus beside us), camera and video phones, texting, sexting, and Twittering to remind us what's out there."[6]

The first lie in the Shame House is this: *I will have more value if I am other.* We have somehow bought into the idea that if we change our looks, our weight, our faces, our everything, then we will at last be worth noticing and "liking." But the truth is so much simpler: *we are created in the image of God, and that alone is what gives us exceedingly great worth.*

Our cultural obsession with celebrity continuously throws fuel on the fire of competition among women. Rather than being encouraged to celebrate our God-designed gifts, strengths, and unique attributes, women are up against ever-increasing pressure to have it all and balance it all, while looking like the end-all. And in a culture that promotes youthfulness and thinness as *the* paradigm of beauty, anyone who doesn't fit the mold can feel like she has little or no value in this world.

The impact all this pressure has on women is startling. Did you know that among women over the age of eighteen, at least 80 percent are unhappy with what they see in the mirror?[8] My heart is broken for the generations of women who have bought the lie that they are not enough—that they have to be *other* in order to have value.

My friends with young daughters tell me the pressure begins so early. Some of their girls (under the age of ten) are already asking how to "go on a diet." This means that in the next couple of years, my future daughters-in-law, who are presently about eight years old or younger, might begin referring to themselves as chubby and ugly. That fact alone should start a righteous fervor in all of us to fight against our shame-driven culture. I'm already praying those little girls discover freedom through Christ and learn to love the skin they're in.

And while I'm on a roll, have you ever considered the insidious names the cosmetic industry chooses for their products? Words like "blur," "cover-up," and "removal" are prominently displayed in most makeup aisles, subtly promoting the shame-lie that women can't be beautiful if they have visible flaws. You want to be attractive and worthy in the world's eyes? Then you'd better hide.

I recently read somewhere that when future generations look at Facebook, they'll wonder where all the women went.

We've replaced images of ourselves with pictures of our children or filtered photos of trees. We are ashamed of our aging, ashamed of the way the seasons of life have changed our bodies. We're disappearing. Here's what my friend Amanda, says: "Shame steals, shrinks, and nips us in contrast with the incomparable freedom there is in filling out the individual 'space' God provides for each of us. Women everywhere sense the pressure to be tiny in bodily size. I think women still have enormous pressure to be small in other ways too, tame and quiet. I know I do. We need to begin stepping into our roles with confidence, and without apologizing for our bodies, or our identities."[9]

I ache for the day we begin to take up space, rather than shrink in shame. How many times have you walked into a room and immediately compared yourself to the women around you? How often have you sat with girlfriends at a coffee shop and ended up complaining about your weight, the calories you consumed that day, your unwhitened teeth, your muffin top, the size of your breasts, or anything else that is lacking or overly abundant? I long to see women celebrate each other, sipping espresso between shouts of, "Cheers to our bodies! Here's to our large pores! A toast to our tummy rolls! Raise a latte to our gifts and talents! Praise God for how he made women!" Who cares if the barista escorts your group out to the sidewalk?

Now look, I'd be deceiving you if I acted like some lady guru on top of Body Image Contentment Mountain, looking down on the pitiable womenfolk who can't live as high above the pop culture fray as I do. No, I'm no master. I'm stuck in the valley with my new friend, Angeline. Oh, haven't I mentioned Angeline? I have a wrinkle between my eyes, and I've named it, okay? I figure if I give the thing a delicate little feminine name, I'll grow to love her. I've tried about a thousand different wrinkle creams on the poor girl. The last one gave me an eye infection. My eyelids swelled up like pink rubber balls, and I had to take two rounds of antibiotics to start looking normal again. I too have bowed to the if-only-I-could-look-ten-years-younger-I'd-finally-be-saved idol.

This is an area in which too many women are wounded. (Meanwhile, the hair, diet, skin-care, cosmetic-surgery, make-up, and perfume industries aren't hurting at all, bringing in a combined total of more than 140 billion dollars per year.) Some of us refuse to wear shorts because we don't want our neighbors to see the cellulite on our legs. Some can be intimate with our husbands only with the lights off. We hate our teeth, so we don't smile in pictures. We've believed for too long that our maturing faces and changing physiques are signs of deficiency rather than evidence of full and meaningful lives.

Trust me. I know how good it feels to exercise and treat your body well, to love your new hair color, to feel beautiful. There's no shame in self-confidence. (You know I'm going to keep sparring with Angeline.) The shame is the thing that drives our insecurity—the belief that those things detract from or add to our fundamental value as women. That's when we fall for the lie that we have to be other in order to have worth.

The Idol of "Otherhood"

The pursuit of beauty, in and of itself, isn't a bad thing. It is actually a divine desire, a holy longing. God is the designer of true beauty, and as such, he is the ultimate expression of it. This is why our souls are thrilled at a powdery white snowfall, the opulent blues of the ocean, or the dark enchantment of a starry night. "We do not want merely to see beauty," writes C. S. Lewis, "though, God knows, even that is bounty enough. We want something else which can hardly be put into words—to be united with the beauty we see, to pass into it, to receive it into ourselves, to bathe in it, to become part of it."[10]

Our longing for beauty is a cry for soul satisfaction. We crave the one person who can actually fulfill us—Jesus. And yet when that hunger does not lead us to him, we end up stepping onto scales of comparison, dancing in circles of insecurity, and riding roller coasters of self-loathing. We convince ourselves the airbrushed representations on the screens around us are the standard of beauty and that we (the millions of us who are not gracing magazine covers or starring in our own reality television shows) somehow don't measure up.

Our cultural obsession with appearance is just another version of the age-old quest to find the fountain of youth, to be immortal. At its best, the pursuit of beauty has the potential to inspire us to worship God for his artistic imprint on our world. At its worst, it becomes the ugliest form of idolatry: the desire to be worshiped, ourselves, as a god. That, my friends, is the idol of "otherhood" in a nutshell. We worship at the feet of the perfection we long for and surrender ourselves to the lies of the beauty-image gospel: all fall short of the glory of the latest supermodel/celebrity/musician.

If only we can be other than we actually are, then we will have achieved perfection. It's a lie that has become so commonplace, so acceptable, that we consider it normal to feel *less than*.

I'm not a person who sees the devil in every challenge, but we so easily forget that the battle we fight against shame is a spiritual one. One of Satan's oldest tactics is to convince us that God is keeping something from us. (He pulled that one on Eve in the garden of Eden.) Shame feeds us those "not enough" lies: you aren't pretty enough, thin enough, youthful enough, fill-in-your-own-blank enough. And we end up swallowing an even greater deceit—that God somehow withheld his love, creativity, affection, and generosity when he created us. That God, in his infinite and infallible wisdom, nevertheless got it wrong when he made us. It's absurd.

Repairing the Foundations

During college, with the help of a 1920s author and some newfound anger, I began to fight back against my own beauty-image shame and repair the cracks in my identity foundation.

At the time, I was dating a self-proclaimed artist (just one in a series of regrettable boyfriend misadventures). He was obsessed with "archetypes of beauty," and he'd go on and on and on and on in this elitist philosophical language about the "lines and curves of the womanly form."

This guy didn't even have the decency to pretend he wasn't checking out other women. We'd be out for dinner or on a walk or something and he'd actually point out female passersby to me: "Look at the way her stomach lays just so. Look at the bend of her hips." In other words, "Blah blah blah." Looking back now, I obviously should have dumped him on his sorry paint palette, but at the time, I didn't have enough sense of worth to even get annoyed.

During the years following the middle-school bus incident, the foundation of my self-esteem became so fragile that by the time I was dating this artist, I could only internalize the sting of his words; if other women had perfect twists and turns, it must mean I lacked them. I bowed down to shame, to the idol of otherhood, believing if I could be other—thinner, more beautiful, more interesting, just different somehow—then his eyes wouldn't wander. I didn't understand my value in Christ, and deeper still, I didn't realize God even cared about my self-image. I mean, he's God. He's got wars to end and diseases to cure. Why would he care about my broken identity, my cracked foundation? Thankfully, I soon learned that God is not only *able*; he actually *desires* to set his daughters free from their bondage to shame.

It's funny the tools God uses to invade our emotional lives. Over spring break that semester, some girlfriends and I traveled to Florida. At the time, I was reading *The Age of Innocence* by Edith Wharton for an English literature class. (Side note: Wharton was the first female author to win a Pulitzer Prize for Fiction. Go Edith!) If you are unfamiliar with the book, here's a quick recap: it's the story of an engaged upper-class couple, Newland and May, whose relationship is threatened by

An Open Letter to the Latest
Media Darling Who Lost All Her
Baby Weight at Warp Speed

Dear Darling,

Let me begin by saying I know you have worked hard to lose your baby weight. I understand it's a challenge of your career to stay in shape. I respect that. I respect you. You have earned your money, your status, and that rockin' post-baby bod. Congrats.

However, I'm having a bit of trouble deciding if your recent weight loss interview is supposed to inspire me—you too can lose sixty pounds in three months!—or turn me into a blindingly angry drooling lunatic. The latter option is winning.

The difficulty, for me, is that when you tell all of America you've gotten back to your pre-baby shape by "working out seven days a week," and that you plan to celebrate all that hard work with a "night out on the town carbo-loading with the gals," it seems you're forgetting to divulge some pretty important information.

For the sake of every woman in our great nation who has ever tried to lose weight, the next time you're interviewed on E! could you at least *consider* mentioning the following people: your chef, your personal trainer, the nanny, the night nanny, your three assistants, the housekeeper, the gardener, your driver, the pilot, your financier, your professional photographer/filmographer who documents your baby's growth, your personal stylist, your hair and makeup person, your agent, and your social media guru who deals with your emails, Facebook updates, Twitter feeds, Snapchats, Pinterest boards, and all the other social networks you're a part of.

When you tell the world how hard you've worked to lose your baby weight, at least *mention* all the little people who helped you get there.

And for the love of all things good, please don't tell me you plan to celebrate your weight loss by "carbo-loading with the gals." I am well aware that some PR person told you to tell me this so that when I am schlepping away on my StairMaster—hours after the weeds have been pulled, and the Play-Doh has been picked out of the crevices in my table, and the Hot Wheels have been put away, and the dinner has been cooked, and the kids have been bathed, and the baby is finally sleeping, and the kitchen is clean, and the budget has been balanced, and the emails have been responded to, and the photos of the baby have been uploaded to Shutterfly—I'll turn on E! to see you unveiling your post-baby bod and I'll think, *Oh, she's going to eat pasta with her gal pals?! Wow. She must be an everywoman. Just. Like. Me.*

I understand that to you, "carbo-loading" means that you *might* put a thin noodle in your mouth and then spit it out before you actually digest the calories. Please at least consider standing in solidarity with all the women who are not a size 2 a mere six weeks after leaving the hospital.[7] It would keep us all from throwing dumbbells at our televisions.

A concerned fan,
Aubrey

scandal when the groom-to-be falls for his fiancée's exotic and mysterious cousin, Ellen. Although Newland and May marry, theirs is a joyless relationship. Newland is disillusioned with his new bride for no apparent reason other than she is *not* Ellen.

So there I was, reading this novel on the beach in Florida, soaking up some much-needed vitamin D after a sunless Chicago winter, when I found myself feeling desperately sad for this imaginary woman, May. Now, it's not unusual for me to relate to a character in a book. The thing that stands out isn't the sympathy I felt for May; it is the *reason* I felt it. I didn't just feel sorry for this fictional character; I felt like I *was* her. Although there was no actual woman stealing my actual fiancé, I understood the sting of losing myself and my identity to an archetype of beauty. I saw Ellen as this unattainable ideal of femininity that I would never live up to, and I saw my roving-eyed boyfriend in the character of Newland.

In the middle of reading this novel, my sadness began to morph into anger. I was irritated with all the Newlands of the world, especially my boyfriend, for being, well, schmucks. I was infuriated by the pressure women are under to squeeze into a singular mold of womanhood. More than anything or anyone else, I was angry with myself. I had allowed shame to write me as an insignificant character in my own life.

My newfound anger was, oddly, a welcome emotion. Like a tough but inspirational coach, anger lit a match in my soul and fired me up to "get out there and make some game changes." Over the next few years, I had much more emotional work to do to fully face my shame, but that year, I finally began the process of overcoming my self-image shame.

First of all, I broke it off with the artist. (Truth be told, he dumped me but then returned asking for another chance. By then, I had built up enough storage of self-worth to say, "Forget you, sucka." That was a nice moment.) Second of all, I joined a confidential care group on campus. Apparently, at my small Christian liberal arts college, loads of female students put themselves under inordinate pressure to behave perfectly, achieve impeccably, and appear flawless at all times. The campus's counseling department took notice and began a support group of sorts for any woman needing emotional restoration.

I attended the group meetings weekly, and although I didn't know the others well (and to protect each other's privacy, we weren't allowed to hang out apart from our weekly gatherings), these women equipped me with courage. They agreed my boyfriend was a schmuck, so I immediately liked them. They also were angry at the cultural pressure women are under, and like me, they were ready to do something about it.

Learning to Laugh

These ladies taught me how to laugh—not in a way that minimized my pain but in the way that gentle humor can sometimes give us perspective. The beauty industry sells us the lie that some young woman with no cellulite, who has been completely airbrushed, is the model of perfection for all of us, no matter our age or body type. Did you know that twenty-five years ago, top models and beauty queens weighed only 8 percent less than the average woman? Now they weigh 23 percent less.[11] This means, even if she wanted to, the average female couldn't possibly achieve the media's modern day version of beauty.

Images of women have been so colored, lighted, and tampered with that we might as well be asked to take our cues from mannequins. It is pretty funny when you step back to think about it. A fake woman has the power to make us feel bad about our real selves? The very idea that we have to measure up to some unachievable appearance is ridiculous, ludicrous, and hilarious. I learned to laugh to take back the power that years of listening to negative beauty-image messages had stolen from me.

Learning to Transform Our Talk

The group also taught me to shut my mouth. We pledged together to abstain from out loud negative self-talk, and although I failed at times (still do), I've stuck to this commitment ever since. We also began to transform our vocabularies. Those who once referred to themselves as "fat" became "curvaceous." The ones who previously complained about having flat-chested "boy bodies" began to refer to themselves as "slender."

Sure, we still had negative internal dialogue, as most women do, but the act of changing the way we talked aloud helped to redefine the way we saw ourselves, taught others how to look at us, and challenged our own notions of what is beautiful. I believe if we can renovate our "body language," and if we can quit pinching the fat of our thighs, sucking in our tummies, and turtle-necking our double chins in front of each other (and in front of the next generation), we can help end the vicious cycle of body-image shame.

Learning Our Roots

After dumping the bad boyfriend and joining the care group, the most significant step I took was to remind myself of my roots as a created being. When shame is attacking, it's difficult enough to wade through the confusing emotions, let alone to stop and remind yourself of the fact that you were designed by God. It's not the most natural thing in the world to sport a cheesy grin and be like, "I feel super ashamed of my appearance right now, but I can handle it 'cause God made me. Yay!"

But truly, if you want to overcome body- and beauty-image shame, if you want to destroy the idol of otherhood, your main task is to understand your foundational identity—to remember, or to learn for the first time, who God is and who he created you to be. Reflecting (sometimes over and over again) on the truth that you are not just some random woman walking around on earth (no!), you are an image-bearer of Christ—that shift changes everything. It is the difference between remaining a secondary character and taking up residence as the heroine in your own story.

Who Are You, Really?

If you have a difficult time answering this question, allow me to assist: you were not created in the image on your screen. You were created as *Imago Dei*, the image of God. You were designed by God to bear his likeness on earth. Unlike other ancient kings and rulers who erected images of themselves in their territories to represent their sovereign presence,[12] God chose to stamp his image on human flesh and blood, sinews and heart.

Now, think about who God is: an artist of the highest echelon, able to bring light from darkness, powerful enough to form the world from nothing, to bring order from chaos. He is the creator of all. God, in his omnipotence, did not have to make you. He could have given life to anyone. He *chose* to craft you into a living being. And when he made you, he pronounced a blessing of goodness over you, just as he did at the beginning of all creation. He looked at all that he had made and called it "very good" (Gen. 1:31).

You—with your specific body type, skin color, facial features, personality, gifts, and passions—are a unique and living reflection of God, designed to carry the image of his love to the world. You were made in his image, but more powerfully still, you were made to be his. You belong to God, not to shame.

In his letter to the church at Colossae, the apostle Paul tells us another thing about what it means to be made in the image of God: "The Son is the image of the invisible God, the first-born over all creation. For in him all things were created: things in heaven and on earth, visible and invisible, whether thrones or powers or rulers or authorities; all things have been created through him and for him. He is before all things, and in him all things hold together" (Col. 1:15–17).

Paul is reminding us that you and I were made by, for, and in the name of Jesus. Because of that, we have an unbreakable identity. You never have to prop up your worth by comparing yourself to others or by attempting to be other. You never have to be a fictional character in an Edith Wharton novel or a Real Housewife. If the pursuit of beauty has become an idol, or if your self-esteem has been eroded by hard times, you can be restored—completely.

As for me, these days whenever I'm tempted to give into those old shameful thoughts—*I am unattractive; I am starting to look old; Angeline is getting bigger*—I try to remind myself of an underwear ad. Let me explain. Victoria's Secret recently ran an ad campaign called "The Perfect 'Body.'" It featured a lineup of ten women with, you guessed it, one identical body type. The internet went crazy, petitioning the company to change the ad, while another underwear company, Dear Kate, created a counter ad featuring a lineup of diverse body types. The tag next to the photo read, "We show the multitude of shapes perfect bodies can take."[13]

The counter ad reminds me that God has indeed created a variety of beautiful women, all designed to reveal his breadth of character and creativity. But it also encourages me that we don't have to take it anymore. We can fight back against the homogeneous beauty images out there. We can post lovely but undoctored photos of ourselves and our friends on Facebook and Instagram. We can display them in our homes. We can upload them to our blogs. If we see advertisements that add to the madness, we can tweet at those companies and express our disappointment. If shame's goal is to shrink us, we can take up more space by using our social media voices. We can show the world what real womanhood is, in ways we've never been able to before.

As you construct your Overcoming Shame Identity, one of the most valuable tools I can equip you with is the truth that you were made with precision and intentionality by the loving hands of God and that, in him, there is power over the world's beauty-image lies. Begin by asking God to speak louder than the negative voices in the world and to tenderly remind you that you are covered—from tummy rolls to stubby toes—in Christ.

And by all means, enjoy the celebrity news (you know I do!) and have fun reading magazines, but turn them off or close them up when they become ridiculous. Get angry when you've had enough. Laugh when you can. And above all else, remember what you're working with—because what you're working with is full of dignity, deep beauty, and abundant worth. The world will be more beautiful when we see the un-ashamed you, because when we see you, we see a truer picture of the glory of God.

DISCUSSION QUESTIONS

1. Which parts of our culture's obsession with appearance or image bother you most?

2. When are you most likely to feel the pressure to be other?

3. How do you and your friends distinguish between a legitimate desire to feel beautiful and being obsessed with appearance or beauty?

4. On a scale of 1 to 10 (1 low, 10 high), how would you assess your level of beauty-image shame?

5. How might your life be different if you had a stronger sense of your great worth and value in God's eyes?

PRAYER

God, I worship you as my powerful creator. I want to experience life the way you intended for me to live it—free from body- and beauty-image shame. Can you help me? Can you remove my insecurities and the pressure I feel to be other? When I feel ugly or unworthy, please tenderly whisper words of your love in my ear. Remind me who I am in you. I am your image, but even more than that, I am yours. In the beautiful name of Jesus, amen.

ZANNA

Overcoming the Shame of Perfect Appearance

Most people would tell you I have it all together. I throw great parties. I have a knack for fashion and decor. And they're right—I do. But for much of my life, keeping up appearances has been more than a fun hobby. It's been an obsession, which began when I was twelve. When my father left, he didn't just leave my mom; he also stopped giving me the special attention he had lavished on me when I was a little girl. That's when a voice began whispering in my ear: *you are ugly, fat, unworthy.* Shame had taken up residence in my heart, launching me into a daily, decades-long battle to be accepted and loved.

During the awkward and vulnerable tweens stage of adolescence, I exchanged my blue jeans and plain white T-shirt for something others would notice. I still remember the elation I felt the first time I walked into a room wearing my favorite outfit. At the time, it was the height of fashion (you might laugh if you saw someone wearing it today): a purple suede suit from JC Penney with a floor-length skirt. The jacket had custom tails. I accessorized it with black leather boots, a black silk blouse, and a black fedora. I looked *gooooood*. Some folks still talk about that suit. I've been hooked on that feeling of standing out and being noticed ever since. If you can turn heads in a room by wearing something incredible, the only thing people around you see is your outfit, not the cracked and fragmented heart underneath.

As an adult, I used to wake up each morning in a silent panic. *Who will I see today? Where must I go? What shall I wear? Whom shall I fear?* I carefully covered my flaws and insecurities by accessorizing my wardrobe.

I'm not exactly sure when things changed for me, but there came a point when God's voice began to overpower the whispering voice of shame. And as I've filled up my heart, mind, body, and soul with Jesus, people have begun to notice more than my outfits; they see what matters most, which is the healing heart underneath.

About a year ago, I walked into a coffee shop wearing an elegant dress and fancy, sling-back high heels. I felt fabulous. Many people commented on my outfit that day, but the comment I remember most came from an elderly gentleman in line ahead of me. He turned around, looked me directly in the eyes, and said, "Young lady, you just light up this room with your smile!" This one compliment was worth far more to me than any of the others because he saw more than what I was wearing. He saw God's light in me.

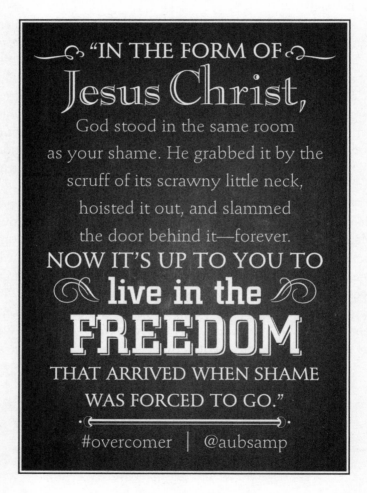

"IN THE FORM OF

Jesus Christ,

God stood in the same room
as your shame. He grabbed it by the
scruff of its scrawny little neck,
hoisted it out, and slammed
the door behind it—forever.
NOW IT'S UP TO YOU TO
live in the
FREEDOM
THAT ARRIVED WHEN SHAME
WAS FORCED TO GO."

#overcomer | @aubsamp

Chapter 3

AN EVICTION NOTICE

Kicking Shame Out,
Some First Steps

SHAME'S LIE: I CANNOT EXPERIENCE
FREEDOM FROM SHAME.

OVERCOMER'S TRUTH: GOD IS ABLE
TO EVICT SHAME FROM MY LIFE.

I was driving home from work one day when I had to pull over to the side of the road because I couldn't see. My sight was impaired by both the rain outside and the tears waterfalling down my cheeks. "Take this from me!" I screamed to God at the top of my lungs. "I hate this!"

At the time, Kevin and I had been married about five years and I still hadn't told him or anyone, really, not even my closest friends, about my experience on the bus or about another secret shame—one I had long buried but that had recently been scratching at the surface of my soul.

During college, as I mentioned in chapter 2, I moved to a healthier place with my body- and beauty-image shame, but because I kept my past shame a secret for so long, I developed an unhealthy, almost obsessive attachment to it. I was habitually fantasizing about returning to my adolescence, to old (and as previously stated, terrible) boyfriends. I wasn't fully present in or grateful for the life I had in front of me. I was mad at myself, but even angrier that no matter what I did, God would not free me from my emotional hell.

It's strange to think back on that time because life was generally good. I don't think people around me would have guessed my inner turmoil. I was leading a student ministry at church. I was mentoring young women. Kevin and I had served as missionaries for nine months in Zambia, Africa. I was living a meaningful existence. But there was always this intangible presence hanging out in the background, in the shadows. And I was starting to believe I would never be free of it.

Taking up residence in the second room of the Shame House is the lie, *I cannot experience freedom from shame*. It's the lie that kept me from believing there was any hope of healing for me—that I could ever have peace of mind and heart, genuinely intimate relationships, and a life free from the burden of my past.

As I sat on the side of the road that rainy afternoon, I felt that elusive presence in the car with me, and I was so tired of it. Shame was moving out of the shadows and into the foreground of my life, claiming too much emotional territory. Before I even recognized it, shame had become my constant companion, a dark and irritating tenant I couldn't evict. I felt like an inmate, and shame had become my guard, locking me inside a prison of depression and distraction, and keeping me from true intimacy with my husband, my best friends, and God.

So I screamed at God. "I hate that you're allowing me to feel this way! I hate that this *stuff* (definitely not the word I used) is still an issue for me after ten years. I hate that I am still clinging to my past. And I'm sick of you not doing anything about it. Please, please, please, please, please, release me from my shame. I can't live like this anymore. Do something!"

It was a pathetic attempt at prayer, full of spite and desperation. No adoration, no thankfulness, no grace. But it was all I had, and it was true. I soon learned that sometimes, even though we clumsily hurl our words at God, even though we pray imperfectly, even though we don't deserve it, in his tender compassion for us, God actually answers. I had no idea he would do so just a few months later.

Kevin and I were in New York City attending a church-planting conference. Well, Kevin attended. I spent the week in the city, taking myself to Broadway shows, pretending to be Audrey Hepburn at Tiffany's, and exploring Chinatown. (I was not—I repeat, I was *not*—looking for knockoff designer purses.) On our last evening there, Kevin invited me to join him for the closing session.

The conference took place in a beautiful old cathedral across from Central Park. Dimly lit and filled with stained glass windows, the space felt like an ancient and sacred portal to New York before the days of modernity. I half expected an angelic boys' choir to magically descend from the ceiling or a dapper newsboy to burst through the doors and jitterbug down the aisles. Unfortunately, the keynote speaker was not much for singing or dancing. He was, however, a well-known but controversial figure in the church, especially regarding his view of women. As a result, I was one of the few females in attendance.

In solidarity with my husband and my sisters in Christ, I sat with Kevin, but I had my arms crossed, fully prepared to throw mental tomatoes. Surprisingly, my defenses melted as this pastor began his message by apologizing for some past remarks. He brought his wife on stage to thank her for putting up with him. I was moved by his honesty, by his affection for his wife, and even more by the stories he shared about taking his girls on daddy-daughter dates. Even though these were just preliminaries and he wasn't yet to the main point of his talk, his comments triggered something in me. Like a soda bottle exploding under pressure, I began to cry.

And let me tell you, it wasn't a dainty cry. I wasn't some *Downton Abbey* duchess dabbing the corners of my eyes with an embroidered handkerchief. No, I was a red-faced, snotty baby wailing at the top of my lungs—in a room full of men who were suddenly staring at me. I had no choice but to stand up and walk out. (If you ever read this, pastor, you know who you are, and I apologize for causing a scene during your message.) Kevin followed me out, dumbfounded.

"Are you okay?" he asked.

"I have to tell you something," I said, "but I am so ashamed to do it."

We sat on the stone steps just outside the church, and I finally confided in my husband that shame was invading every corner of my life, including our sex life. After five years of marriage, everything just poured out of me. I confessed to Kevin my fixation with the past, my flagging sense of self-worth, and my anger toward God and myself. Through tears, I told him about the incident on the bus and eventually about my other secret shame. When I finally finished talking, I had to catch my breath. It felt like I had run a marathon, the emotional equivalent of a 26.21875-mile journey.

Kevin was silent for a time, thoughtfully taking it all in. After several moments, he placed a hand on my knee and asked if he could pray for me. I was resistant at first. I felt so defenseless in that moment. Something as intimate as prayer caused me to bristle against it, to wish I had never said anything, to want to run away. But God was keeping me nailed to those steps.

As Kevin prayed over me, I experienced prayer in a new way, like hearing the way your name sounds in a foreign accent—familiar and fresh, all at once. His was not a desperate prayer like my roadside tantrum had been. But it wasn't eloquent either. It wasn't even an "ask" of God, really. It was a simple declaration of truth: "Jesus, you are love, and you love

Aubrey. She is haunted by shame. I know that. You know that. I adore this woman. But my feelings for her are nothing compared with how you care for her. She needs to surrender her shame to you. You want to set her free."

It was exactly what the thirteen-year-old girl in a training bra on the bus needed to hear and believe.

The next day, as we walked through New York City (by that point, thankfully, my crying had become less ugly), we ended up at Ground Zero, the site of the September 11 attacks on the World Trade Center. At the time, construction on the memorial was just beginning, and there was still a chain-link fence around the perimeter. Loved ones and visitors had left hundreds of thousands of notes, stuffed animals, flowers, pictures, and poems. It was a messy confusion of grief and love, a nation's imperfect attempt to console itself. To this day, I would say it remains one of the most powerful things I have ever seen. The people of New York were healing from a tragedy they never deserved, never invited upon themselves. But there it was—New York City embodying the truth that there can be beauty in brokenness, even after the very worst has been thrust upon us.

I know better than to compare my personal pain to that of a national tragedy, but it was there, in that city whose people were bravely beginning to heal, that God finally began to set me free from shame.

Kicking Shame Out

The following list includes some of the first meaningful steps I took in my attempt to surrender my shame to God. It would be amazing if I could tell you something like, "Follow these four easy steps and you too will be free from shame!" As I'm sure you know, overcoming shame is not like that; it's a journey. And I don't know if your journey will look like mine. I do, however, know this: as you begin surrendering your shame to Jesus, he is ready and able to evict its control from your life.

1. Share Your Story

Scripture tells us that Adam and Eve were created without shame (Gen. 2:25). Did you catch that? We were created to exist unashamed. But we all know how the story goes. In the garden, God's beloved children wanted to be "like God" (Gen. 3:5). As a result, Adam and Eve (and you and I) were filled with sin and shame. They attempted to hide that shame by covering themselves with fig leaves. But they couldn't hide from God.

The consequence of their sin was banishment from the garden, but before they left, God revealed his compassion. "The LORD God made garments of skin for Adam and his wife and clothed them" (Gen. 3:21). He removed their fig-leaf outfits and clothed them with his restorative grace. God lovingly covered Adam and Eve's shame with his mercy, a foreshadowing of the ultimate kindness that would come to all of us, to all of our sin and shame, in Jesus.

I'm telling you this because shame loves to keep us hidden in our pain. Shame flourishes in silence. But just as it did for Adam and Eve, God's mercy draws us from our hiding places.

When I first opened up to Kevin that evening in New York, on the one hand, it was like being found after a long game of hide and seek. It felt so freeing to finally be seen and known. On the other hand, it was like being found *out*, being caught. Often, the big scary thing lurking beneath our shame is a fear of rejection or abandonment. If you are deeply known—if you let them see the real you—your loved ones may think differently about you. They might even discard you. I was so nervous Kevin would be angry that I had never told him my story. I was scared he'd run in the opposite direction.

That didn't happen, thankfully, but the simple act of talking to Kevin helped me realize something: even if Kev ran for the hills, even if he never looked at me the same way again, it would have been painful, yes, but it would not have diminished my value. My worth is not found in my husband. And it's definitely not found in my past. I may be sinful and ashamed, but I am clothed in the restorative grace of God, and my value is found in him.

Talking to a loved one about the shame you may have been hiding is a powerful step toward experiencing God's kindness. Sharing my story with Kevin was the defining moment in evicting shame from my life. God helped me to open up to him, which in turn empowered me to tell some close friends, who encouraged me to talk with a Christian counselor, and now, years later, I share my story with women's groups, at retreats, and during ministry events. Every time I tell the story of how God set me free from shame, I experience more emotional freedom and have the amazing privilege of watching God set others free from their own shame. When you bring your story to the light, shame can do nothing but recoil from the brightness.

2. Sever Unhealthy Connections

When Kevin and I returned from our New York City trip, one of the first things I did was to begin untying myself from unhealthy connections to the past. I deleted toxic "friends" from Facebook. I gathered shame tokens I had been holding onto—photos and mementos from past relationships, souvenirs, old journals—and threw them out with the recycling. For years, I had held onto these tokens thinking they had value, that they told the story of *me*. In truth, they only chained my soul to shameful memories. I said a physical goodbye to the shame from my past in order to birth new life in my present. I thought about burning these keepsakes in a big bonfire, but I wasn't sure how environmentally friendly that would be. Plus, I like to imagine that my painful past has been recycled into something cool like will.i.am's headphones or Banksy's spray-paint cans.

If there are any unhealthy relationships or reminders of those relationships in your life, destroy them. If you've been in a toxic relationship, but you're hanging on because you are afraid to disappoint that person or because you feel too emotionally attached, let that person go. If you are controlled by anything—if anything in your past or present is inviting shame in—ask God to help you begin evicting it. It won't be easy, I know, and you won't be able to do it alone, but shame's stronghold in your life isn't worth it. When you refuse to let shame take up any space in your life, it is forced to pack up and move out.

3. Seek Help

Every summer, Kevin and I spend a week at a family member's lake house. It's a place where our boys can be boys—they fish, collect tadpoles, throw rocks into the lake, and run around barefoot and muddy-toed. One afternoon on a recent trip, I tried to convince the guys to leave the bug collecting for a bit and cruise the lake with me on a WaveRunner. Nobody was interested, so Kevin tossed me the keys. "This is your chance for freedom. Go!"

I ran down to the dock, as excited as a little kid digging through her Halloween candy. I jumped on the WaveRunner and started the engine, anticipating the thrill of the wind in my hair, the sun on my cheeks, and the water spray on my legs. But there was a problem. I couldn't get it off the dock.

I tried rocking back and forth, but it wouldn't budge. I climbed off the dang thing and pushed it with all of my might. But no, it wasn't going anywhere. So I stubbornly climbed back on. *Fine. I will just sit here and enjoy the sun.* I tried to be content in the moment, but there was an adventure waiting for me and I was missing it. Finally, I ran back to the house and asked Kevin for help. He gladly obliged, pushed the WaveRunner off the dock (he's so manly), and I zoomed away. I drove around for almost an hour, woo-hooing when I bounded over large waves, laughing when paddlefish leapt across my path, and waving at my boys on the shore as I cruised past.

We miss out on the adventure God has for us when we settle for the spiritual or emotional equivalent of sitting alone on the dock. We might spend years wrestling with shame in our own strength and never experience any real change. That is why God has given us the gift of trained Christian therapists—to help us get off the dock and enjoy the adventure of a healing journey.

When we returned from that New York City trip, I began seeing a wonderful counselor. She not only listened and offered wise guidance; she also prayed for me. She helped me to silence the critical voices in my head.

I'll never forget, in the height of my struggle with shame, someone asked me a completely benign question about a clothing store. It was something as simple as, "Do you like to shop there?"

It was the most nonessential question in the world, but I full-on panicked. Did I like the store? Or didn't I? I didn't know, but I also didn't know how to simply say so. I didn't know how to express ambivalence or mixed feelings. Shame rushed over me like a tidal wave, and I felt like a little kid doggy paddling my way to the surface. Together, my counselor and I created a vocabulary list of feeling words so I could reclaim my voice. Learning to express my inner reality was like learning to swim with confidence. She also gave me permission to discover the music *I* liked, the books *I* wanted to read, the things *I* cared about.

The point is that finding a good professional can help you recover the parts of yourself that years of listening to shame have stolen. You are worth it.

4. Disagree with Shame

As I yelled at God and knuckled away tears that rainy afternoon in my car all those years ago, he brought to mind a verse that had been among my favorites as a teenager: "Therefore, there is now no condemnation for those who are in Christ Jesus" (Rom. 8:1). I had a Bible study leader once who pounded that verse into me—literally. During one of our weekly gatherings, she repeated the verse five times in a row while persistently (and yet, somehow, sweetly) pounding her fist into my thigh. "There is now no condemnation for those who are in Christ Jesus. There is now no condemnation for those who are in Christ Jesus. There is now no condemnation for those who are in Christ Jesus. There is now no condemnation for those who are in Christ Jesus. There is now no condemnation for those who are in Christ Jesus." I knew I had allowed shame to condemn me for far too long. I was finally ready to return the favor—to condemn the shame that held me prisoner.

Satan uses shame as a weapon to demoralize us, and for years, I agreed with his accusations of "Aubrey, you aren't capable enough. You aren't a good enough wife and friend. Aubrey, you aren't strong enough." But ever since that day in New York City, whenever shame creeps back in, trying its best to condemn me, I condemn it right back—by disagreeing with it. Aloud. (If you ever catch me doing this, you'll probably think I've gone crazy.) If I have those shame-filled thoughts, I will stop and actually say something like, "I don't agree with that, in the name of Jesus. Jesus says I am enough, in him."

Disagreeing with shame refutes it and refuses to give it power. On the next two pages is a chart I created, both for myself and for the groups I speak to. It's a retaliation tool, in a way, so that when shame starts accusing, you can be prepared to fight back with these scriptural truths.

Is there a shame accusation that stands out to you? Is there a Jesus statement you might have at the ready whenever shame creeps in? Whenever you fight shame with a tool as powerful as God's truth, Satan's argument has no platform on which to stand.

As you begin sharing your story, severing unhealthy connections, seeking help, and disagreeing with shame, you'll find that God is bigger, badder, and more robust than shame could ever hope to be. It's not even fair to make that contrast, because God's love is so opposite from shame's condemnation;

If Shame Says...	I Disagree Because...	Jesus Says...
I do not belong.	I disagree because...	I am the apple of his eye. I am his. He has called me by name. He will never leave me alone. He has given me a community and special gifts to offer to it (Ps. 17:8; Isa. 43:1–2; 1 Cor. 12:12–31).
I am nothing special.	I disagree because...	Before I was even born, God chose me to be his daughter (Eph. 1:4–5).
I am a mistake. I am not good enough.	I disagree because...	He has created me with power and wonder. That is true no matter how life changes me (Ps. 139).
I missed the mark.	I disagree because...	His power is made perfect in my weakness. In his name, I can own my imperfections and even grow in maturity. In him, imperfection does not equal inadequacy (2 Cor. 12:7–10).
I am the sum of my mistakes.	I disagree because...	In him, I am never covered with shame. He makes everything beautiful in its time. I am a new creation; the old has gone; the new has come (Ps. 34:5; Eccl. 3:11; 2 Cor. 5:17).
I deserve to be treated with disrespect. I will give my heart to anyone who comes along.	I disagree because...	God is my daddy. I am a daughter of the King, and a coheir with Christ. I deserve to be treated like one (Rom. 8:15–17).

I should be other than who I was created to be.	I disagree because...	He has created me uniquely in his image (Genesis 2).
I am unlovable and alone.	I disagree because...	Nothing can separate me from his love. Because he loves me, I can learn to handle any situation (Rom. 8:35).
I cannot count on anyone.	I disagree because...	I can cast all of my burdens, cares, and anxieties on him. He cares deeply for me (1 Peter 5:7).
I will never be able to move past this.	I disagree because...	When shame condemns me, he is greater than shame, and he will help me (1 John 3:20).
There is no purpose for my life. I am trapped. The best life I will ever lead is one in my fantasies.	I disagree because...	His plan for my life is bigger and better than I would ever be able to design for myself. He can do immeasurably more than I can ask or imagine (Jer. 29:11; Eph. 3:20).
There's just too much brokenness to overcome.	I disagree because...	He doesn't just heal my brokenness (although he does that); the broken places actually become a catalyst for beauty and a tool he can use for his kingdom. The ways in which he's comforted me, I can use to comfort others (2 Cor. 1:3–5).
I will never be accepted for who I really am.	I disagree because...	He will never abandon me. He will never leave me, nor forsake me (Deut. 31:6).

God frees, while shame imprisons. The two are so contrary in nature they shouldn't even share room in the same sentence. Nonetheless, in the form of Jesus Christ, God stood in the same room as your shame. He grabbed it by the scruff of its scrawny little neck, hoisted it out, and slammed the door behind it—forever. Now it's up to you to live in the freedom that arrives when shame is forced to go.

DISCUSSION QUESTIONS

1. If you've never shared your story before, what keeps you from opening up to a loved one or close friend? What might be holding you back? If, on the other hand, you feel comfortable with vulnerability, what do you attribute to helping you share with others?

2. If you feel comfortable, share an example from your own life of a moment you've felt afraid of rejection or abandonment.

3. Think about the unhealthy relationships in your past or present. What emotional or physical tokens are keeping you connected to that person? If you were able to release those, what difference would it make in your life?

4. What intrigues or intimidates you about the idea of going to see a therapist? If you have been before, what was your experience like?

5. When you think about shame's accusations, what words or phrases come to mind? What does shame say to you? If you could say anything in response, what would it be? How can you condemn shame?

PRAYER

Dear Jesus, thank you for hearing my prayers, even the imperfect ones I pray when I am frustrated and overwhelmed. Please help me to know what it would look like to surrender my shame to you. Please give me the courage to begin living in the light of your freedom. I need you to empower me with your strength to fight back against shame. Please evict shame from my life, because I recognize I can't do this without you. Amen.

DIANA

Overcoming the Shame of Attraction

I like wearing dresses to church. It's a habit my parents instilled in me at a young age. Although I rebelled and wore pants for a few years in my teens, I've since come to love wearing special clothes for church and wear a dress most Sundays. The only challenge I have is that modest dresses seem increasingly hard to find. So I have to put a lot of effort into finding clothes that are appropriate, but still cute. Everyone wants to be attractive, right?

However, attracting the wrong kind of attention can quickly turn the warm fuzzy of feeling cute into a hot flush of shame. I don't know if this has happened to you, but I have often attracted the wrong attention from men who are married and significantly older than me.

I was visiting a church one Sunday and felt confident that I was modestly dressed in short black heels and a loose-fitting dress with a high neckline and a hemline just slightly above the knee. When I walked up to the front doors, two of the three male greeters insisted on giving me a hug. An older man wearing a wedding ring struck up what I thought was merely a friendly conversation and then proceeded to touch the small of my back twice while forcing small talk.

Even though I was thoroughly covered and acting appropriately, I felt ashamed, like this was somehow my fault, that I had worn something I shouldn't have or behaved flirtatiously. But I hadn't! There's a legitimate shame you feel when you do something wrong, but then there's the confusing shame you feel when something wrong is done to you. I had no idea how to process this kind of shame.

I was taking my cues from my feelings, that I must have done something wrong if I felt shame, but two biblical truths helped me see things from a different perspective. The first truth was written by the prophet Job: "If I am guilty—woe to me! Even if I am innocent, I cannot lift my head, for I am full of shame and drowned in my affliction" (Job 10:15). Shame is experienced by the guilty and the righteous alike. The second truth is similar: the gospel writer affirms that God "sends rain on the righteous and the unrighteous" (Matt. 5:45). This means that God's goodness is also experienced by the guilty and the righteous alike.

This knowledge that my circumstances are not always my fault has helped me to navigate confusing experiences of shame that came from receiving the wrong kind of attention from the wrong kind of men. I've learned that God didn't create me to have shame, especially not over other people's actions against me.

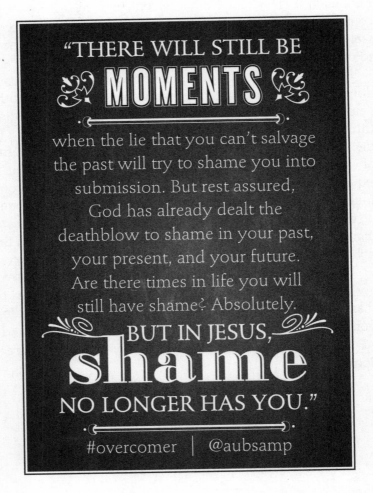

"THERE WILL STILL BE

MOMENTS

when the lie that you can't salvage the past will try to shame you into submission. But rest assured, God has already dealt the deathblow to shame in your past, your present, and your future. Are there times in life you will still have shame? Absolutely.

BUT IN JESUS,

shame

NO LONGER HAS YOU."

#overcomer | @aubsamp

Chapter 4
TENDING TO THE BROKEN PARTS

The Shame Game-Changer

SHAME'S LIE: MY PAST IS UNSALVAGEABLE.

OVERCOMER'S TRUTH: GOD HELPS
ME RELEASE THE SHAME IN MY PAST.

It wouldn't be right if I wrote a book about shame without telling you my whole story. Stuff's about to get real up in here. Let's begin with *Endless Love*.

I don't know whether you saw it, and I'm not sure I could comfortably recommend it. The 2014 remake of the 1981 movie about teenage lovers was more of a tween clothing-store commercial than an actual film. Let's be honest, the thing was a total cheese-fest, a sensational and saccharine story about star-crossed adolescents, and a completely unhealthy portrayal of romance, as most teenage love stories are. Nevertheless, I paid good money to see it with a friend. Okay, I may have seen it more than once. Alright, alright, I loved the stupid thing. (I've already confessed my *Real Housewives* fangirlness. I don't know why I'm trying to pretend my movie sensibilities are more refined.) Give me a chick flick any day of the week. #suckedrightin.

On our drive home from the theater, my girlfriend and I reminisced about old boyfriends, first loves, and the ones who got away. Sadly, most of the ones who got away were never ours in the first place. My friend admitted to having harbored a secret crush on the same boy since fourth grade. The kid didn't even know her name until their high-school graduation.

I confessed my starry-eyed tendency to project deep meaning onto any and every interaction with a boy. If my crush of the moment happened to walk past me at school—even if he never spoke to me, even if he never looked at me, even if he avoided me on purpose—I just knew the only reason he could possibly have for doing so was because of his romantic feelings for me. *He must have ignored me because he doesn't want me to know how desperately he loves me.* Right, because that makes a whole lot of sense.

As mom to three sons, I now feel great compassion for those poor clueless boys. I thought they were so much more self-aware and plotting than they actually were. In fact, they had no idea the effect they were having on me. However, not all the males I encountered during those endless love years were clueless. When I was a junior in high school, my boy craziness led me into a relationship with a man who was fully aware of what he was doing.

There was a significant age difference between me and the restaurant manager at my after-school job, but I considered him a friend. Unfortunately, things became too friendly one afternoon when he called me into his office for a meeting and locked the door behind me. I'll spare you the details, but I will tell you this: even now, twenty years later, I still battle shame when I think about the time I spent behind those locked office doors. This very moment, I'm struggling with the proper words to express what happened. I'm tempted to write something benign like, "I was in an improper relationship with an older man who was my boss." However, part of waging war against shame means refusing to sweep my story under the rug, so I will write only words that are true. I was not merely in an improper relationship with an older man who was my boss. I was sexually abused by him—repeatedly.

That experience was such a dark secret that I repressed the memory of it for the next decade. God helped me make great strides in my emotional growth during that support group in college and after opening up to Kevin in New York City. I had finally broken free from some of shame's major strongholds in my life. But at twenty-seven years old, my past still had a grip on me and I feared it would forever control my future. I wanted so desperately to live a vivid existence, completely untainted by shame. I was closer than I had ever been, but I had no clue how to begin healing from this one final piece—my past. Then something happened that became a shame game-changer, giving me a newfound nerve, the guts to face and repurpose my past.

I got pregnant.

The third lie residing in our Shame House is this: *my past is unsalvageable.* I still don't know whether it was the grace of God, my newfound maternal instinct, or just the reality that another human being was about to dramatically invade my existence (probably it was all three), but I determined that year to retroactively kick down those office doors. I was going to do whatever it took to begin a new future. I was going to live the truth: *God helps me release the shame in my past.*

(I want to stop here and acknowledge that the world of pregnancy, infertility, and miscarriage can bring up a whole other realm of shame for women. If this is an area of pain for you, I am so sorry for your struggle.)

As I mentioned before, I wish I had some straightforward process to offer: *You too can be free from the death grip of your past in no time at all!* I can't do that, but I can show you three measures that helped me come to terms with my past. I call them Brain Retrain, Shamer Release, and Self Revisits.

Brain Retrain

I wasn't exactly sure how to begin working through the pain in my past (a slightly huge undertaking), but I knew enough to know that the best way to kill a habit is to starve it, and some of the shame I was clinging to was definitely habitual. Experiences in my past may have planted the shame seed, but I was the one who had tended to my shame and allowed it to blossom into this wild thing. I knew I had to somehow root it out.

Growing up in church, I probably heard about a thousand sermons on taking my thoughts captive and making them obedient to Christ (2 Cor. 10:4–5). This wasn't a novel idea to me, but until that year, I had never actually put those sermons into practice. I had never before taken control of my own thought life and had, almost by accident, allowed it to control me. Like a twisted Sam-I-am, memories persistently pursued me, and I entertained their presence. I knew it was time to stop.

Here's what I did. Let's say I started daydreaming about an old boyfriend or my boss, as I was wont to do. I began to instantly halt in my mental tracks and say a little prayer. "God, I'm thinking of this person again. But I'm moving on now, so get him outta my head. Make my thoughts obedient to you."

At the beginning, this wasn't the most polished or even spiritual of exercises. I'd have to force myself to start thinking of something else, anything else, to reorder my thought life. I'd plan pretend vacations to Disney World. (I know that is some people's version of torture, but I happen to believe it *is* the happiest place on earth.) I'd think about my Christmas shopping. I'd count imaginary steps or make mental lists of things I was thankful for. I was doing whatever I could to retrain my habitually unhealthy thought patterns.

Over time (and this wasn't one of those twenty-one-day quick fixes, mind you), my thoughts wandered to those painful places less often. I remember sweeping my kitchen floor one afternoon, not that long ago, when it occurred to me that it had been such a long time since I had obsessed about my

"Shameless" Scripts

As you face your shame from the past, your mind may cling to some old, negative thought patterns, such as:

I don't matter.
God can't love me.
Something is wrong with me.
How can I be such a [fill in the blank]? I should be more [fill in the blank].
I am bad/unworthy.
God will never forgive me.
I don't belong.
I am always going to struggle with [fill in the blank].

One practical way to transform these thought patterns is to rewrite them with a Shameless Script. These are statements designed to help you experience less shame. Here are some examples:

God gives me value. I am enough.
I'm God's beloved, and I will not abandon myself.
God created me. Therefore, I am not a mistake.
I will stop punishing myself.
God calls me beautiful. I am his.
God forgives me; I will forgive myself.
God will never leave me nor forsake me.
I am God's, and he is making me more like him every day.

You can develop your own Shameless Scripts using whatever words convey grace to you. Maybe you already have a life-giving motto. Or perhaps you are empowered by a line from a favorite song or a Bible verse. (Chapter 8

> includes a list of verses that deal specifically with overcoming shame.) Once you have your script, write it down and post it in places where you will see it often. Type it into your smartphone. Tape it to your bathroom mirror. Paint it on a coffee mug. Heck, write it on your arm with a ballpoint pen if you need to. Do whatever it takes so you're prepared to respond when shame starts the trash talk.

past. I couldn't actually remember the last time I "remembered." God had retrained my brain, so to speak. Now my thoughts were more often in the present than they were stuck in the ugly fantasyland of my past (not to be confused with the lovely Fantasyland at Disney World).

Shamer Release

At four months pregnant, belly deep in brain retraining, I waddled through the aisles of my local Christian bookstore, stopping at the women's studies section, hoping there'd be some resource to help me deal with the residual shame from my past. I came across a book called *Every Woman's Battle* by Shannon Ethridge. I picked it up, thumbed through the pages, and thought it looked interesting. But for some reason, I set it back down and walked out of the store without purchasing anything.

Here's one reason I am certain God loves and pursues his daughters: I could not get Shannon's book out of my mind. I'd be in church and someone would mention it. I'd see ads for it online. The bookstore even sent me a catalog with their featured titles, and guess what was on the cover? God was practically screaming at me to read Shannon's book. The crazy thing is (and I've always responded with a mix of skepticism and envy when I hear other people tell stories like this) when I finally gave in to God's insistence and returned to the store to purchase the book, I had the exact amount of money in my wallet necessary to buy it, coins and all. If this were an *Endless Love* story, I'd say it was meant to be.

By the time I finished the first chapter, I understood the reason God wanted me to read it. Shannon's book deals with sexual and emotional fulfillment and freedom from the past. God used her words to untie my old crusty bandages, clean and rub ointment over my wounds, and mend the remaining injuries. Her words healed me. I didn't know then that I was reading the work of a woman who would become my future writing and speaking mentor and a big sister figure. (But first things first; I'll come back to that later.)

When I finished Shannon's book, a section on surrendering stood out to me. "Why do we continue beating ourselves up?" Ethridge asks. "Why do we allow our misery to affect our mental and physical health? You don't have to carry all that emotional baggage."[14]

I later discovered that Shannon, as part of working through some childhood neglect and abandonment issues, decided to do for herself what her parents hadn't been able to do. She spent a summer taking herself on outings she had longed to experience as a child—she took herself to the movies, out for ice cream, and to the mall for Godiva chocolate. She even enjoyed an afternoon of journaling in the sunshine while on a picnic at the zoo. Shannon now coaches other women to "put on their big girl panties and deal with their own emotional issues." This encouragement is easy for her to give to others because she first learned how to do it herself.

Shannon once wrote in an email to me, "I had two choices. I could be bitter toward my parents for being too busy and distracted to pay much attention to me growing up, or I could carve out time to focus on my own emotional needs and minister to the hurting little girl trapped inside this grown woman's body. I chose the latter, and my entire family dynamic is much better for it."

Like Shannon, I realized I had a death grip on misery that I did not have to be carrying, and I also had two choices. I could hold on to the past and continue allowing those who'd hurt me to shadow my life, or I could release them. But releasing my grip on the past meant I had to do something I was not excited to do—forgive those who had shamed me.

I was bitter at my boss and those boys on the bus, resentful that they had stolen goodness and innocence from me. I thought if I forgave them, if I truly surrendered it all, then I was giving them permission to hurt me again. I mistakenly equated forgiveness with accepting their behavior. In time, though, I was able to experience what Bible teacher Beth Moore describes about her own healing journey: "I finally had to turn over some of the hurts of my childhood to God's sovereign authority because I realized they would consume me like a cancer. Once I began to surrender to him in this painful area, God began to give me a supernatural ability to forgive."[15]

When I began the work of forgiveness by surrendering my anger to God, it wasn't like I was suddenly and supernaturally okay with the abuse I had suffered. But I was able to take small steps that helped me eventually to see my experiences—and my shamers—differently. When it came to the boys on the bus, I simply began to pray, "God, teach me to forgive," and over time, I began to have a small but sincere dose of compassion for them. Don't get me wrong—I don't believe "boys will be boys" or some other nonsense like that. But as I've gotten older, I've realized that it was likely an adult who taught those kids that it was okay to treat girls like objects. They may have even experienced abuse themselves. I hate what they did, but I was able to release my bitterness by mustering some grace for them.

As for my former boss, an adult who knew better, I found it much more difficult to release him.

Do I still believe he acted sinfully against me? Yes. Were there days I fantasized about taking revenge against him? Definitely. Were there moments I had to forgive him over and over again? Absolutely. Even now, his actions still anger me. But they don't control me. I have come to understand that forgiving our shamers does not mean we accept their hurtful behaviors or that we permit them to continue. It doesn't mean we have to maintain or reestablish a relationship with them. Frankly, they may not even need to know that we have forgiven them.

When you think about forgiving your shamers, never equate it with ignoring truth, trivializing pain, or denying the past. Think of it instead as an active, ongoing work of the Holy Spirit and as a continual looking to the cross. If you are struggling to understand what it means to forgive someone who has shamed you, these clarifying statements about what forgiveness is and is not might help:

Forgiveness Is Not . . .	Forgiveness Is . . .
Ignoring the truth	Admitting that what happened to you warrants forgiveness
Engaging in a relationship with your shamer	Defining personal and relational boundaries in connection with your shamer
Giving permission for harm or wrongdoing	Pursuing your own freedom and health
Denying your pain	Opening your heart to healing
Trivial or cheap	Costly
Denying the past	Letting go of the past to move toward a better future*
A quick fix	Ongoing
A feeling	A choice
Always reciprocal	Possible even if the shamer never knows about it
For your shamer	For you
Always deserved	A loving response to the forgiveness you've received through Jesus

* Sandra D. Wilson, *Released from Shame* (Downers Grove, Ill.: Intervarsity, 2002), 158.

To forgive those who have shamed us, it helps to remember that we ourselves have been forgiven: "But God demonstrates his own love for us in this: While we were still sinners, Christ died for us" (Rom. 5:8). That's what it means to continually look to the cross. We do not forgive our shamers because they deserve it or even because we know it's "the Christian thing to do." We do it as a humble response to the love and forgiveness we've undeservedly received in Christ. The result is astonishing, because releasing our shamers releases us from their grip.

This year my oldest son will turn nine, marking almost a decade since I began to hand my shamers over to God's authority. I rarely think about them anymore. Yet even so, if they do cross my mind, I am able to genuinely practice forgiving the boys on the bus *and* my former boss. I hope that God invades and transforms the brokenness in their own lives.

Self Revisits

One of my closest friends is a gifted therapist. Kathy often says, "To truly heal from shame as an adult, we have to go back and give our child self what she needed but never received: nurturing, empathy, the truth in love. Our inner little girl needs to know she is God's beloved."

For me, ministering to the little girl inside meant facing her again. It may have been those pregnancy hormones operating on overload, but something gave me the gumption to return to the restaurant I worked at all those years ago. (I would not recommend this for everyone, especially if it feels like it would do more harm than good.) I had this impression that if I could experience myself now, as a grown woman, in the space where I was that hurting girl, God would somehow reveal himself to me in a new way.

Keep in mind, I was living nearly fifteen hours away, was married, and was preparing for a new baby. I was also ubersick, as morning sickness for me lasts all day, all nine months.

This wasn't a convenient experiment, but I felt the Holy Spirit illuminating the path to my past, and I wanted to follow.

As I drove into the parking lot, I immediately recalled the scent of my boss's office, a nasty mix of cheap cologne and French fries (which did not help the aforementioned morning sickness). I remembered the Beatles poster on the wall and the dark wood paneling that needed whitewashing. I could envision his desk and his executive toys: the silver pendulum balls, the office minigolf green. He even had a World's Best Boss mug (the most inaccurate mug in the history of all mugs ever made).

I parked my car in front of the building and walked in. By then, it had been converted into a tween clothing store and looked nothing like it had all those years ago. Skinny jeans and hipster hats occupied the space where the office used to be. Still, I felt a bit shaken. This was where I had let myself be taken advantage of, where I returned again and again to a boss who held so much power over me. This was the place where I kept a secret, the place that kept *me* a secret and hidden in shame for years.

As I wandered through the racks of clothing, part of me wished the restaurant had been transformed into something more symbolically meaningful like a flower shop or a church. I wanted to grasp hold of something concrete to signify my redemption. Instead, I realized it didn't really matter what this location had become because God had restored *me*. I had been released and redeemed. I was no longer the girl behind locked doors. There I stood, in the middle of a store designed for girls in their own *Endless Love* years, realizing I was no longer captive to the shame I had experienced in mine.

I sat in the parking lot afterward and had a good long cry. I cried for my seventeen-year-old self. I cried for my stolen dignity, innocence, and self-esteem. I cried for how long it took me to tell anyone. I cried because I never stopped it from happening. I cried for all the losses. But then I was crying because

Tamar, the Daughter of David

One of the most disturbing and tragic stories of shame in the Bible is about King David's daughter, Tamar, who was raped by her brother. Scripture tells us Tamar removed her ornamental robe, the symbol of her status as a virgin daughter of the king. In its place, she put ashes on her head and spent the rest of her days in mourning (2 Samuel 13). It's a devastating story of how shame can destroy a life. This young woman had her dignity, purity, and future stolen from her, and her own father did nothing. He failed to secure justice on her behalf. Although our stories may look different, all women can imagine Tamar's heartache, loss, and shame. I, for one, want to reach into the pages of Scripture, wrap a blanket around Tamar, and whisper words of tenderness into her ears. I want to lift up her chin, brush those ashes out of her hair, and help her come out of mourning.

I sometimes wonder if the prophet Isaiah had Tamar in mind when he prophesied about the Savior to come: "The Spirit of the Sovereign LORD is on me, because the LORD has anointed me to proclaim good news to the poor. He has sent me to bind up the brokenhearted, to proclaim freedom for the captives and release from darkness for the prisoners . . . to comfort all who mourn, and provide for those who grieve in Zion—*to bestow on them a crown of beauty instead of ashes, the oil of joy instead of mourning, and a garment of praise instead of a spirit of despair.* . . . Instead of your shame you will receive a double portion, and instead of disgrace you will rejoice in your inheritance. And so you will inherit a double portion in your land, and everlasting joy will be yours" (Isa. 61:1–3, 7, emphasis added).

> Her earthly father may not have rescued her, but I cannot wait to see Tamar in the presence of her heavenly Father. I imagine she's strutting around heaven, a beautiful crown instead of those ashes. A garment of praise instead of that torn robe. Her shame replaced with radiant, everlasting joy.

there had also been a gain. I speak with so many women who know they've been set free from shame in Jesus, but they are unable to say goodbye to that last tiny piece of the Shame Identity, because they can't forgive themselves. That day, I was able to forgive myself for clenching so tightly to my past for so many years. God helped me open my hands.

As I released the last of the shame that had taken up residence in my life, something else moved into its place. Although I couldn't quite name it yet, whatever this change was, it felt big and explosive, but it was the opposite of an earthquake. It was as if I had been walking on a tightrope my whole life, always this back and forth tipping, a constant teetering. Then suddenly, a sturdy platform had emerged underneath me. Or maybe it was always there, and I just finally looked down long enough to recognize it. Either way, my footing was now sure and strong. I didn't have a name for what was happening, but as I look back now, I know what God was doing. He was replacing my shame with his solid and dependable joy.

In Chicago, we have these nasty winters, and when I say nasty, I mean after a few months everything is covered in muddy slush. Your pants, boots, and even your socks are perpetually and maddeningly wet. Your car and your home become sludge-covered and salt-stained messes.

If you've ever lived in a snowy part of the country you know that even in the midst of a record-breaking ugly winter, anytime a fresh layer of snow falls, the once-muddy slush, now newly cleaned, will sparkle with sunlight. One of my favorite parts of winter is seeing this snow-dazzle phenomenon at night. There's not much more beautiful than moonlit snow shimmering like the stars above it. Once, my five-year-old son, clad in his warm footie pajamas, shook me awake in the middle of the night. "Mom!" he gasped excitedly. "You have to get up and look outside! There are diamonds in the snow!"

Letting go of the shame in my past was like waking up to discover that something new had finally arrived in the darkness. What once felt like it would never be more than a stained and messy piece of my story was now covered in a new belief: God can make all things, even the darkest and ugliest places in us, sparkle with beauty.

I returned home from that trip and began what felt like a new life. I've followed Jesus since I was eleven years old when I heard Elvis Presley's stepbrother tell his life's story about being touched by two kings: the king of rock and roll, and the King of kings. I marched down the aisle of that old-school Southern Baptist church revival meetin' and asked Jesus to be *my* King. (I still have a special affinity for Elvis, by the way.) But following that visit to my past, I had a renewed ability to worship God freely, to walk with him without restraint, to minister to other women out of a newfound joy, and to dive into and teach the Bible with passion. I enjoyed my relationship with Kevin like I never had before. (Wink. Wink. Sorry. I can't help myself sometimes.) I was able to be present in my friendships and with my family more than I ever had been before. Nothing I was doing was particularly new. I was basically in all the same roles. The difference was that now I was unfettered by shame.

Just a few weeks after that final stop-off in my past, I gave birth (after thirty-six excruciating hours) to my first son. I loved him with a fierceness I didn't know was in me. (I still do, but he's old enough now to be like, "Mom, stop already!") His presence didn't remove my pain. In fact, having children brought on a whole other gamut of it. (That's a topic for another book.) But when I saw those chubby cheeks, touched those tiny toes, and smelled that syrupy-smelling baby head, I was reminded of God's faithfulness. He is a good and perfect parent, caring for us more deeply than we could ever care for ourselves.

The prophet Isaiah beautifully describes God's faithfulness to restore our shame when he declares, "Do not be afraid; you will not be put to shame. Do not fear disgrace; you will not be humiliated. You will forget the shame of your youth and remember no more the reproach of your widowhood. For your Maker is your husband—the LORD Almighty is his name—the Holy One of Israel is your Redeemer; he is called the God of all the earth. The LORD will call you back as if you were a wife deserted and distressed in spirit" (Isa. 54:4–6).

Your road may look different from mine, but there is no need to fear or be controlled by your past, because God is faithful to find and restore even the broken pieces you have left behind. There may be moments when the lie that you can't salvage the past will try to shame you into submission, especially as you begin your own version of retraining your brain, releasing your shamers, or revisiting your past. But rest assured, God has already dealt the deathblow to shame. Are there times in life you will still have shame? Absolutely. But in Jesus, shame no longer has you.

DISCUSSION QUESTIONS

1. What would it look like for you to make your shameful thought patterns obedient to Christ? In what ways would you like to be able to "retrain your brain"?

2. If you could say something to shamers in your past without fear of being hurt again, what words would you say?

3. When you read the descriptions of forgiveness, which statement is most helpful to you? Which one is the most difficult for you to believe?

4. What does it mean to you, personally, to minister to "the little girl inside"? What words or actions would she find encouraging?

5. If you feel comfortable, share a mistake from the past or another area where you'd like to experience self-forgiveness.

6. How might your life look different if you were able to surrender the pain in your past?

PRAYER

Almighty God, I praise you for your ability to overcome the darkness in my past. Please open my eyes now to see your hand throughout my life, even during the bad stages. Help me release my tight grip on the pain from my past. Help me let go. Help me to forgive. Help me to overcome so that I can experience a life of fullness and freedom in you. Amen.

RACHEL

Overcoming Daddy Shame

I grew up as a preacher's daughter in a small town in Massachusetts. I was a daddy's girl through and through. He was my hero, and I was his biggest fan. We got along great when I was little, but things began to change about the time I reached seventh grade.

Things at home were hard. My mom and dad fought throughout their entire marriage. But come Sunday morning, no matter how much screaming had gone on the night before, my mom dressed my three younger siblings and me in our Sunday best so we could go to church and hear Dad preach from the pulpit about faithfulness, love, marriage, and how to be a better parent. This is when my double life began—we lived one life at home and another in public. It didn't matter what happened behind closed doors, as long as we didn't talk about it.

In eighth grade, I became severely depressed. I cried every morning before school, and I was crippled with anxiety. I was popular and had lots of friends, but it didn't matter. I was dying inside. At the end of the year, I was sexually abused by another student. Word spread like wildfire that I had hooked up with this guy, and I blamed myself for the whole thing. I entered high school with a tarnished reputation and a longing to rebel. I started drinking and hanging out with older students. My dad came home from work one afternoon to find me with an eighteen-year-old guy when I should have been in school. He did nothing. A month later, he caught me drinking. Again, he did nothing.

We moved from Massachusetts to Missouri halfway through my freshman year, when my dad took a job at a new church. I was insecure at my new school and instantly hated everyone and everything. Throughout the remainder of my high school years, I continued to drink a lot and throw myself at guys.

One night during my senior year, my parents had an especially bad fight. My mom came into my room afterward and told me she was going to ask my dad to move out. A few months later, my mom decided I should know the truth since my dad had made no effort to tell me himself. He had been having an affair for the last two years with a woman from our church.

Weeks before my high school graduation, my dad moved out, and we were left with all the broken pieces. He lost his ordination and was eventually diagnosed with narcissistic personality disorder, which explained his inability to see all of the pain he had caused.

I didn't speak to my dad for over a year. I went to therapy for a short time after the divorce. My therapist asked me to describe the loss of my relationship with my father. I told him that's just what it was, a loss. He was dead to me. The daddy that was my hero didn't exist anymore; he never had. I was so embarrassed for having had such a strong desire to please him. I never wanted to be called a daddy's girl again.

After years of verbal and emotional abuse, I experienced silence for the first time—from the fighting, from my friends, from the church, and from God. I was alone. I was determined to cling to God throughout this ordeal, but I kept screwing up. I would never measure up. I desperately wanted the approval of others. I felt judged and abandoned by almost everyone from my past. I went off to college and continued to reach out to men and alcohol to fill the silence. My double life was at its peak. My drinking soon turned into experimenting with drugs, but I maintained a 3.9 GPA, so on the outside, it looked like I had it all together.

I didn't know who God was to me anymore. Prayers that started with "heavenly Father" made me cringe, so he couldn't be my father. I didn't know what to believe. My dad had been my pastor for eighteen years. Could I believe anything I had learned about God from him? All I knew was that I desperately wanted healing. I was ashamed of the woman I had become. I wanted to stop living a double life, because it was exhausting. Little did I know there were people who loved me and were praying for me.

One friend from high school was particularly persistent. Through her friendship, I began to turn back to God for the first time in three years. I heard Louie Giglio speak at a conference during my senior year of college. He said something that dramatically changed my life: "The cross was enough for you."

Those words brought me to my knees in prayer. I had thought my mistakes and my screwed up life were too much for God. I didn't think he could do anything with me anymore. I had undermined and belittled what Jesus did on the cross for me. But it was enough. I accepted the love of a heavenly Father that night. Nothing I had done in my past could keep me from him. I knew the changes wouldn't be easy, but I simply prayed that God would open and transform my heart. I finally allowed him to fill the silence in my life.

Forgiving my dad is a daily act. He continues to fail me every day, and he will never be my hero. But sometimes I don't think our earthly fathers deserve that place of honor. And it's okay. They're far from perfect. Without the experience I had with my dad, I would never know what it's like to cling to God with every fiber of my being. I am enough for God, and *he* is my loving, redemptive Father.

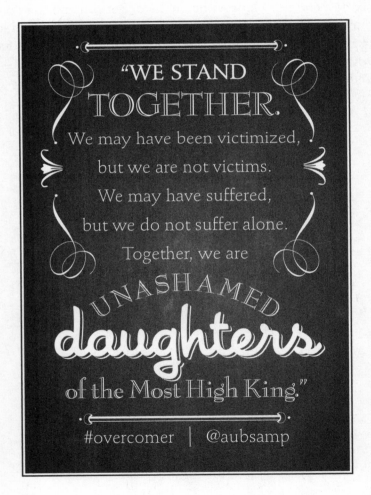

"WE STAND TOGETHER. We may have been victimized, but we are not victims. We may have suffered, but we do not suffer alone. Together, we are UNASHAMED daughters of the Most High King."

#overcomer | @aubsamp

Chapter 5

WELCOME TO THE NEIGHBORHOOD

Conquering Shame in Community

SHAME'S LIE: I HAVE TO
FIGHT SHAME ALONE.

OVERCOMER'S TRUTH: WITH THE
HELP OF MY COMMUNITY, I CAN
COURAGEOUSLY OVERCOME.

I grew up in in the South, where the arrival of any snowfall, even a light dusting, triggers an apocalyptic fever, an end-of-the-world panic. Upon hearing reports of a looming snowstorm, shoppers race to the store to stock up on milk and bread, knowing the roads will be rendered useless for days. Malls close down. Doctor's offices shut their doors. Churches cancel services. And school, to the bliss of southern children everywhere, is immediately called off.

In the Midwest, where my kids are growing up, school cancellations don't happen so easily. Snow days are hard won, like a fighter's prize. If school is going to be canceled, winter can't be halfhearted; it has to come in like a supervillain wielding dangerously low temperatures and hurling down inches and inches of snow before people will even consider running inside to hide. We're tough here in Chicago. Snow? Cold? Do your worst.

I have to roll my boys out of bed on school days. But on snow days? It's like a prison-break scene. They wake up early, jittery from joy, itching to hash out plans. They start calling their buddies in anticipation of what the day, this treasure of a day, free from the tyrannous tedium of school, might hold out before them.

If temperatures are semibearable, my kids will wrap themselves up—a mummification process of putting on snow pants, boots, coats, hats, gloves, and scarves—to go play outside before they've even touched breakfast. Soon all of the little neighborhood mummies, equipped with shovels and sleds, will gather in our sloped back yard to create what they call the ultimate sledding hill. (It's actually pretty tiny, but to their little eyes, it is the biggest sledding hill in the history of the universe.) Cheeks chapped with cold, hearts beating with exhilaration, the neighborhood kids all erupt in screams of delight as they give each other the courage to face the sweet terror of the plunge.

Sometimes one of my sons will venture outside again later in the day, long after the other kids have gone inside to sip hot chocolate and thaw. He'll usually return about five minutes later. "What happened?" I'll ask. "Did you change your mind?"

"It's not fun without the whole neighborhood, Mom," he'll sigh.

Vulnerability in Community

There is childlike joy to be had when we are willing to step outside—to talk about our shame openly—with others. I know from experience how difficult it is to practice vulnerability. Anytime we feel ashamed, on any level, the last thing we want to do is broadcast those feelings to the world around us. Shame loves to isolate, and isolation loves to keep us from experiencing the benefits of community, which is why we need to address the fourth lie in the Shame House: *I have to fight shame alone.*

Perhaps you feel like the only one who has ever dealt with your specific brand of shame. You believe you're the only one who has ever wanted to escape your life, so you keep that thought to yourself. Maybe you're the only one in your group of friends whose parent walked out on her, so you think no one could possibly understand your ongoing fears of abandonment. Perhaps you feel like the only one suffering financially, the only one who battles loneliness or insecurity, the only one in a difficult relationship, the only one with an addiction. When we feel like we're alone, opening up about our inner conflicts is all the more terrifying.

Hiding is a natural response, as old as the garden of Eden. We all need to feel safe and comfortable with people before we can even think about baring our souls before them. But far too often, we believe the lie that our imperfections equal our inadequacy, and that exposing our flaws will reveal spiritual immaturity or lack of faith. So we suffer silently, saying nothing about our inner pain. All the while, there is greater freedom and deeper joy to be had when we are willing to reveal our authentically flawed selves. It's ironic, actually. As we disclose our weaknesses to one other, that act actually strengthens us and our communities to continue overcoming shame. Acts of vulnerability produce contagious courage.

Years ago, I experienced a profound moment of coming out of isolation and overcoming shame in community when I attended a women's weekend with a group of thirty writers. Although the purpose of our first evening together was to share our life stories, I decided at the onset of the session not to share mine. At the time, I had never talked openly with anyone outside of Kevin, my intimate group of friends, and a counselor about my past, and here I was among women whose obvious gifts, accomplishments, and advanced education left me feeling intimidated. As these women went around the circle courageously telling their stories, the shame tapes were playing loudly in my head. *You are not good enough. You'll never really be a part of this community.*

A Community of COURAGE

I mentor an amazing group of young millennials. We call ourselves The Sundays. Over the years, they have taught me so much about being intentional in relationships because they fight to have meaning in theirs. They're sick of having only shallow acquaintances, so they are ready and willing to go deeper with each other and with God. As their leader, I often ask them to pause and evaluate our little group. How are we doing? How are things going? Are we meeting our goals? Somewhere along the way, I developed the acrostic COURAGE as an evaluation tool for us. Because I want our group to be one that practices courage in community, we are learning to assess ourselves based on the following definition and questions.

A community of COURAGE is:

Christ-centered: Are we keeping Jesus at the center of our time, discussion, and study?

Overcoming: Are we empowering each other to overcome life's challenges?

Unashamed: Are we allowing shame or Christ to define us as women?

Restorative: Are we doing whatever it takes to restore any relational brokenness that might exist within the group?

Authentic: Are we being honest and real about our flaws and struggles?

Growing: Are we maturing spiritually and emotionally?

Encouraging: Are we lavishing love and pointing each other to Christ?

We know we're never going to live up to this acrostic perfectly; that's not the purpose. But as we evaluate ourselves, we can make adjustments to our group based on COURAGE. And as we keep these values at the forefront of our minds, we are regularly reminded to ask God to continue transforming us into a community of courageous women.

The evening progressed and I realized I was the only woman in the room who hadn't spoken and everyone knew it. I had two options: I could either boldly take my turn or allow my silence to make things super awkward. My heart began to pound so hard I had to press my hand onto my chest to quiet it down. *Help me!* I whispered to the Holy Spirit.

After mumbling excuses about tiredness and lack of preparation, I took a deep breath, stared hard and long at the floor, and began to share my story—the bus, the boss, the emotional pain, the residual shame.

When I was done sharing that night and looked up, every single woman in the room was crying. One by one, they walked over to me, placed a hand on my leg or shoulder, prayed, and spoke words of comfort and encouragement. They became for me what author and priest Henri Nouwen has written about: "Still, when we ask ourselves which person in our lives means the most to us, we often find that it is those who, instead of giving much advice, solutions, or cures, have chosen rather to share our pain and touch our wounds with a gentle and tender hand."[16]

My community that weekend wasn't offering me advice or solutions. With their attentive presence and compassion, they were showing me the heart of Jesus. This was one of the scariest things I've ever done, but breaking out of my isolation was ultimately so rewarding. By speaking up, I took another step toward shutting shame down, and I forged a bond with these amazing women, one we still have today. They became my sisters that evening. The separation I once felt—the "they're better than me" intimidation—no longer existed. That experience may have benefited me, but I was not the only one. As we dared to give and receive our stories, we fought shame and created a courageous community together.

Jesus, Shame, and Community

The courage and freedom from shame I experienced at that writers' retreat reminds me of a biblical moment; one in which Jesus transformed the shame of his own community. You might know the wedding story from John 2. A couple of newlywed kids run out of wine on their big day. What you might not know is that running out of wine at a wedding was not just a little embarrassing oversight by the caterer. In a culture that placed exceedingly high value on hospitality and honor, running out of wine would have been a shameful situation for this young couple—a social disgrace, an insult to the guests, and even a bad omen. In his commentary *John for Everyone*, New Testament scholar N. T. Wright puts it this way: "The family would have had to live with the shame of it for a long time to come; bride and groom might regard it as bringing bad luck on their married life."[17] The bride and groom, their family, and even their guests would have felt the repercussions of this shame.

Jump with me for just a minute to the Old Testament, all the way back to the words of Isaiah, because this is cool. Foretelling of the Messiah to come, the prophet declares: "On this mountain the LORD Almighty will prepare a feast of rich food for all peoples, *a banquet of aged wine—the best of meats and the finest of wines*. On this mountain he will destroy the shroud that enfolds all peoples, the sheet that covers all nations; he will swallow up death forever. The Sovereign LORD will wipe away the tears from all faces; he will remove his people's disgrace from all the earth. The LORD has spoken" (Isa. 25:6–8, emphasis added).

Now back to John 2. On the third day of those wedding festivities, Jesus not only revealed his glory with a miracle; he removed the newlyweds' shame by changing ordinary water into the finest of wines. His actions fulfilled Isaiah's prophecy and foreshadowed an ultimate third day to come—his resurrection triumph over death.

When Jesus turned water into wine, it wasn't only a strategic miracle to jump-start his public ministry. It was a sign of the day his body and blood would become the bread and wine of salvation, swallowing up death, removing the disgrace of his people, and transforming all things forever, including our shame. One of the things that amazes me about this moment (I mean, there are so many amazing things; how can you pick just one?) is that Jesus performed this miracle in the context of a community event, a wedding party, no less.

He didn't take the bride and groom behind the DJ's booth and pour them a lone glass of wine; he poured his overcoming-shame blessing all over the entire wedding party. Jesus certainly works in our personal lives in special ways—he has done so powerfully in mine—but he also wipes away the tears from *all* faces, as Isaiah said, and removes the disgrace of his *people.* Jesus removes shame in community.

I'm mentioning this to you because sometimes Christians place such a large emphasis on our *individual* walks with God, our *solitary* quiet times, and our moments of *private* worship. Which, don't get me wrong, are beautiful practices. But we must remember that the Christian life was never meant to be lived alone. We are a more faithful, more enduring, and stronger people when we experience the joy of Jesus in community. Like the women at that retreat, we overcome shame more powerfully when we do it together.

The joy that Jesus brought to the bride and groom that day, and to their surrounding community, must have been so incredible! Can you imagine being on the brink of utter reputation-ruining shame, only to have it erased? And not only removed but also transformed into something wonderful that everyone around you can also enjoy? It brings to mind another retreat experience where I had the privilege of watching firsthand as shame was renovated into joy.

Kevin and I were leading a young adult retreat together. On the second day, we split up. The guys went with Kevin to talk about manly stuff like chopping down trees and growing beards, or whatever guys talk about on retreat. The women were with me. Our plan was to discuss that ever-elusive question of balance, but the Holy Spirit was moving powerfully in another direction, and we ended up devoting our time to sharing personal experiences of shame.

These brave women sat in a circle of chairs and opened up about seeing themselves as failures, as dumb or uncool, weak, unconfident, and awkward. Some considered themselves ugly ducklings or the fat girl in the room. Others shared secret questions they were asking about their sexual identities. Some talked about long-term battles with mental or physical illnesses and addictions and about the resulting fear that they were freaks. This was a group of some of the most brilliant, talented, and successful women I ever have been around, and each one felt like she was alone in her shame journey. But as each opened up, something miraculous happened: no one was alone anymore.

Although each shame story in the circle was unique, these women constructed a common bond, an understanding, an acceptance of one another. They were overcoming their individual shame as one. As they released secrets and shame they had always held onto out of fear of being known, they received nothing but love and compassion from one another.

If there had been banners hanging around the room, they would have read something like, "We stand together." "We may have been victimized, but we are not victims." "We may have suffered, but we do not suffer alone." "Together, we are unashamed daughters of the Most High King."

At the end of the session, all the women moved to the center of the room. With the help of another leader, we laid hands on and prayed over them. When the men rejoined us at the end of the session, they took one look at our eyes, puffy from crying, and asked, "What just happened in here?" We couldn't help but laugh! It was as if a heart surgeon had simultaneously opened each one of us up, cleaned out our clogged arteries, and put us back together with more power pumping through our veins than ever before. We laughed because we were reveling in our brand-new strength of heart, our newfound joy.

Grab a Sled

It's one thing to put yourself out there at a retreat setting, away from the realities of life. It's a whole other challenge to exercise vulnerability on a regular basis with your day-to-day community.

What gets in the way of finding joy in our everyday communities? If Jesus overcomes shame in community, why aren't we all experiencing that freedom? Unfortunately, as we too well know, our Christian communities sometimes fail us. Too often, there is a gap between the biblical ideal of Christian community and the less than ideal reality we experience. If you've ever been part of a faith community, chances are you may have already been hurt or felt judged by it.

Sometimes we hide from community because we're intimidated. Maybe there's this amazing group of women you'd love to be friends with, but you think, *They're more confident than I am. They don't struggle the same way I do. They're much stronger spiritually.* And you let those perceived differences keep you from stepping out of your house, grabbing a sled, and joining in the fun with them.

Some of our isolation is because of shame. We allow it to seclude us, to prevent us from ever being fully seen, known, and loved. We mistakenly believe we have to clean ourselves up or get our act together before we can really invest in others.

Shame keeps us locked up on the inside, forced to always watch others enjoy the benefits of community, while never permitting us to encounter it for ourselves.

I know it can be difficult. Shame may have robbed you of self-confidence. Perhaps you're an introvert or a person who struggles with social anxiety, and so it isn't especially natural for you to put yourself out there. There are a lot of reasons to avoid opening up to your community. However, doing so can break down barriers and assist everyone involved in finding further freedom from shame.

At the end of the day, vulnerability doesn't have to be overly complicated, excessively dramatic, or heavily programmed. The most powerful moments I've experienced in community are the organic ones when one woman talks about a struggle and another woman says, "Oh, I struggle with that too, but I never came to you because I assumed you had it all together."

Consider a tiny first step—ask God to provide an opportunity for you to share your story with a safe group of people. Then a second step—ask him to give you the mettle, when that opportunity comes, to open your mouth. (Sometimes starting is the scariest part.) If you can harness the courage to grab a sled and join the neighborhood, it's so worth it. My guess is that your community will be much improved with your perfectly imperfect presence in it.

Last but Not Least: Sexual Shame and Community

I've chosen to write about sex in this chapter because this is another area in which shame would like nothing better than to keep us isolated. If we're going to overcome something as formidable as sexual shame, we need a courageous community to help us.

My friend Cindy Johnson addresses the complex nature of sex and Christianity in her book *Who's Picking Me Up from the Airport?* Cindy writes, "When we talk about sexual purity without hearing a person's story, it takes a very emotional and physical experience and reduces it to a simple mistake they made or a sin they committed. It communicates that this one act makes them a bad Christian. It turns people away from Jesus. It turns people away from forgiving themselves. It turns people away from the idea of waiting."[18]

I don't know your story. But I do know that no matter what it is, you are loved deeply and accepted fully by Jesus. Nothing you do will ever undo his love for you. Nothing you can abstain from doing will ever earn it either. You are loved. Period.

At the end of the day, God cares about our actions and choices, but he is not concerned with legalistic behavior modification. God wants to transform our hearts so that he becomes the object of our devotion and worship. The results of which will positively and genuinely change our lives. As Johnson says, "I believe God is far more concerned with carefully and delicately handling the whys and where to go from here than getting into the whats (what you have or haven't done and with whom)."[19]

A single friend of mine recently began to realize her why. She was motivated to have sex because she was looking for a way to gain acceptance and approval from the men she dated. These men always ended up dumping her and breaking her heart. And she was sick and tired of it. In her own words, "I just feel like I've haphazardly given away all the control of my body and my heart. I want to reclaim it."

So she's made a new decision—to wait to have sex again until she gets married. I think her choice is respectable, but it's also super countercultural. She's told a couple of her very close friends in confidence, but she's honestly ashamed to tell other friends and family because she knows they'll be like, "YOU DID WHAT?" (I think she probably needs to find a better community. I mean, haters gonna hate.)

Another one of my fabulous single friends sent me this text message expressing her own experience of shame and sex: "Growing up in church, I was constantly reminded that sex should be saved for marriage. I still feel shame and guilt for making the decision to have sex when I really was not ready. I wanted to please my stupid high school boyfriend at the time. Now that it has happened, it's difficult for me to sit back and say, 'Well, I believe sex should be saved for marriage,' because I don't want to be a hypocrite. I feel like a loser if I tell people I've suddenly decided to hold out for 'the one.'"

The point is that on either side of the coin, sadly, our sex lives (or lack thereof) have the potential to make us feel ashamed. I alluded to this in previous chapters, but I'll just be vulnerable with you now (gotta practice what I preach). Kevin and I waited, with much anticipation, to have sex until we were married. So I was completely unprepared for when, during the first few years of our marriage, I often wouldn't want to have sex with him. Kevin was kind and patient, but as you can probably guess, shame didn't go so easy on me. I felt like a failure as a wife and as a woman, really. Prior to getting married, I seriously imagined I'd be a love machine. I just knew Kevin and I were going to do it *all the time*.

As you know, our sexuality is so connected to our emotional world, making it especially complicated. It wasn't until I felt safe being emotionally intimate with Kevin about my past that I finally felt free to really enjoy physical intimacy with him. The act of vulnerability revitalized our sex life. (When we tell this story to friends, Kevin usually throws in a "Yeee-aaaah baybay!" or starts singing the chorus of Pharrell's "Happy.")

No matter your story, I want to remind you again (in case I haven't said it enough) that you are God's deeply loved daughter. If you've been hurt, confused, or led astray when it comes to your sex life, and if you've been carrying all of that shame by yourself, take a step out of seclusion by talking to your spouse (if you're married), a close friend, a trustworthy pastor, or even a small group of emotionally-safe people. You'll soon discover that God cares for every part of you—your heart, your soul, your dignity, and your body—the whole package.

God has given you the gift of community—with all of its quirks—so that you don't have to fight shame alone. In choosing to be vulnerable with that community, you'll foster emotional freedom for yourself and help to cultivate a culture of courage for others. Your once-desolate winter can be transformed into a celebratory snow day—something that's much more fun when you're with your neighbors.

DISCUSSION QUESTIONS

1. What hinders your ability to engage in community?

2. How would you describe your experience of Christian community? Has it more often been a source of shame or a source of healing from shame? Why?

3. On a scale of 1 to 10, assess your willingness to be vulnerable with others. What is the scariest thing about opening up to other people? What is the most satisfying thing?

4. How do you respond to the idea that overcoming sexual shame requires being in community? Is that something you feel drawn to or something you'd rather avoid?

5. If community gives us the courage to continue overcoming shame, how would you say that's been true in your experience? How can you give courage to others?

PRAYER

God, thank you for never leaving me alone. Even when it feels like I'm the only one, you have given me the gift of friendship to remind me that I'm not. Please help me to choose courage and to engage in community even when I'd rather hide. Walk beside me and help me walk beside others with vulnerability. Help me to experience more of your love and freedom from shame as I do. Amen.

CALLIE

Overcoming the Shame of an Unwanted Pregnancy

From the moment I saw the positive pregnancy test, I was angry with God. We had planned on having a few carefree years as newlyweds before getting pregnant. We wanted to pay off student loans, travel, and live abroad. I had dreams of graduate school and a career. Less than eleven months after my husband and I were married, our son was born. The baby changed all our plans.

As strongly and swiftly as I felt the anger rise, so too did shame. We didn't want this baby, and I felt a mix of horror and disgust at my own selfishness. Every pro-life mantra I had ever heard now seemed like an accusation. "Children are a blessing from the Lord!" So why couldn't I change my attitude and feel elated with this pregnancy?

My intense shame over not wanting my baby was a heavy burden only my husband was privy to. I was sure no one else could understand. While others celebrated the fact we were going to have a baby, my husband and I couldn't bring ourselves to do so. Shame bred silence, and silence bred isolation, turning the whole experience into a vicious cycle. We felt alone in the world and engulfed by shame.

When our son was born, healthy and beautiful, we fell in love with him. It took time, but our love for that baby brought healing to our raw emotions. Yet even in the midst of loving him, I still carried the shame of initially having not wanted him. Now that I adored him, I was even more appalled at how much I hadn't wanted him. Was I even worthy of being his mother? How could I look into that sweet, trusting face each day remembering how I felt when I found out I was pregnant?

Since the shame lingered after our baby's birth, we still kept silent. People knew bits of the story, of course. We might mention offhand that our son had been a surprise baby or that we'd planned on waiting longer before having children. But it wasn't until a friend pressed me on it that the entire story spilled out, complete with my shame.

Our babies toddled around her living room as I told her the truth. Amazingly, my friend didn't reject me. For so long, I'd believed I'd be reviled if anyone knew our story, but my friend listened without judgment. She showed me compassion. She led me in prayer. She encouraged me to repent of ingratitude and to ask God to remove the stain that shame had tattooed onto my soul. When I lifted my head after that prayer, I had my first shame-free taste of motherhood.

Later, my husband and I shared the story with our small group at church. We were no longer in hiding. Looking into the faces of people we loved, we realized again that our fears of rejection had been unfounded. They accepted us. They challenged us. They pointed out areas where we still needed to grow. Our honesty brought a new intimacy with our friends.

I was emboldened because I was finally living free of secrecy and shame. Best of all, my story has given me opportunities to help others. When friends have felt mired in shame, I've been there to listen. I wrote an article on the topic and was amazed to see how many people related and responded. After knowing the grip shame had on our lives and remembering how it isolated us, it is a joy to help others walk toward a life free of shame.

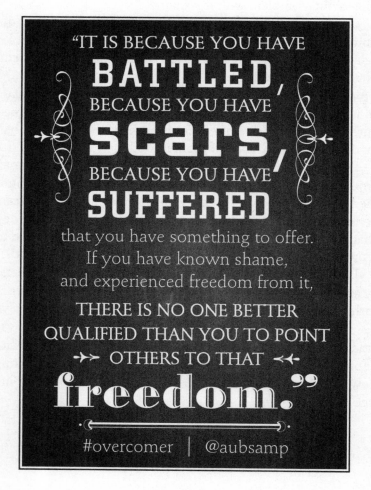

"IT IS BECAUSE YOU HAVE **BATTLED,** BECAUSE YOU HAVE **scars,** BECAUSE YOU HAVE **SUFFERED** that you have something to offer. If you have known shame, and experienced freedom from it, THERE IS NO ONE BETTER QUALIFIED THAN YOU TO POINT OTHERS TO THAT **freedom."**

#overcomer | @aubsamp

Chapter 6

ROOM FOR WORK AND PLAY

Transforming Pain into Purpose

SHAME'S LIE: I AM NOT GOOD
ENOUGH TO BE USED BY GOD.

OVERCOMER'S TRUTH: GOD
TRANSFORMS MY SHAME INTO RADIANCE
AND MY MISERY INTO MINISTRY.

It's time for a short quiz! Don't worry. I promise there are no trick questions, and I won't ask you anything you don't already know. How's that possible? Because the quiz is about *you*! Circle the answer that best represents your response, or write your own answer in the space provided next to "Other." Then sit tight with your responses. We'll come back to the quiz at the end of the chapter.

1. Overall, how would you characterize your gifts and talents?

   a) I'm a creative type.

   b) I'm a good listener.

   c) I'm gifted at seeing the big picture.

   d) I'm great at inspiring others to get behind a new vision.

   e) Other:_____

2. When do you feel most energized?
   a) When I'm helping others behind the scenes
   b) When I'm onstage or in front of an audience, teaching or encouraging them
   c) When I'm spending quality time with God and others
   d) When I'm in nature
   e) Other:_____

3. Which statement best summarizes your personal motto?
   a) You don't need a lot to enjoy life.
   b) You can triumph over anything.
   c) Healthy relationships are the keys to a happy life.
   d) Work hard. Play hard.
   e) Other:_____

4. What issues are most likely to prompt an "it's not right" response in you?
   a) The abuse of women and children
   b) A friend in emotional pain
   c) Global poverty and injustice
   d) Other:_____

5. What would you say has been the most difficult season of your life?
   a) My childhood. I still have a lot to work through.
   b) Junior high and high school. No brainer.
   c) My first years of marriage were unexpectedly difficult.
   d) Now. This is one of the most stressful seasons of my existence.
   e) Other:_____

6. If you could go back in time and offer advice to your younger self (knowing now what you wish you knew then), what would you tell her?

   a) Step away from the perm.

   b) Dump that loser.

   c) Let it go.

   d) This will make you stronger.

   e) Other:_____

7. If you could design your dream job, what would it be?

   a) I'd care for others through civil service, education, or by advocating for the voiceless.

   b) I'd do something creative: write, make art, style hair, design clothing, decorate homes, something to express myself.

   c) I'd start something—a business, a ministry, a team, a family.

   d) I'd join a goodwill or missions organization and travel to help people around the globe.

   e) Other:_____

The Best-Qualified Candidate

For years (since before we attended that church-planting conference in New York City ten years ago), my husband, Kevin, has felt called by God to plant his own church. In the past whenever he talked about it, I always mentally brushed it aside: *Oh, what a silly dreamer I married.* Even when he began researching church-planting residencies a couple of years ago, I was still in denial.

If you haven't gathered it by now, "change" and "going with the flow" aren't exactly my strong suits. (I can't even type those words without using quotation marks.) I am generally scared of the unknown, and when Kevin was exploring residencies, denial was the only way I could deal with the fact that I was terrified of what becoming church planters might mean for our family. For a number of reasons, church planting was a difficult concept for me even to wrap my head around, let alone get excited about.

For ten of the twelve years we had been married at that point, Kevin and I had served in leadership roles at a wonderful church in the Chicago area. Kevin was a full-time pastor for eight of those years. I led the junior high ministry, taught at retreats, and spoke at other ministry events, including "big church." Our sons had only ever known one church. They loved their friends, Sunday school teachers, and the free hot chocolate. How might they react to our leaving? Would I find my place in a new church body?

Given my aversion to change, you can imagine something as significant as leaving our church, moving our kids, and losing our financial stability was not exactly my cup of tea. But those were mostly excuses. Hidden beneath all my fears were some shame questions. *What will people say? Do we really have what it takes to plant a church? What happens if we fail? What will everyone think?* I was listening to another one of shame's deceits, the fifth lie in the Shame House: *I am not good enough to be used by God.*

It was a tense season in our marriage. (Warning: I'm going to refer to my husband as "Keviepoo" in the next sentence, so when he reads this chapter, he'll remember what a sweet and doting wife I am.) Keviepoo was being pulled by God in one direction: *Go! Plant a church!* I was holding tightly to the reins and pulling in a non-direction: *Stay! Are you crazy?*

When we reached out to a mentor couple for guidance, they encouraged us to attend a weeklong church-planting assessment. The purpose of the event was to encourage and observe potential candidates as a means of assessing their capacity for leading a church-planting team. The couple thought it would help guide our conversation and assist us in discerning whether this was something God was calling us to do. We agreed and arranged to attend a few months later.

When we arrived at the assessment, my husband began referring to it affectionately as "This Awesome Church-Planting Boot Camp." Because *The Hunger Games* was already taken, I dubbed it "The Torture and Agony Games," T-TAG for short.

Looking back, my less than enthusiastic attitude may not have been entirely the assessment's fault. Had I looked at the online description, I might have avoided a gross misunderstanding about the structure of the event and shown up a little better prepared. I had packed my bags for a couples getaway, expecting heart-to-heart counseling sessions, exercises in communication, and glasses of water with cucumber slices floating in them. Instead, we were thrust into group projects, late-night brainstorming meetings, and strategy sessions, all while being monitored and appraised by clipboard-toting assessors.

Being in a fishbowl of analysis was disconcerting, to say the least, and it again brought out some of my well-worn shameful thoughts: *What makes me think I am capable of leading anything? Am I relevant anymore? Why am I even here? I don't think I have what it takes to be used by God as a church planter.* As I wrapped myself in an ever-tightening web of insecurity, my husband soared. He was voted MVP by most of his assessors, while I rarely even ranked on their charts. (T-TAG, I tell you.)

Convinced I wasn't measuring up to some elusive wow factor, I attempted to cover my feelings of inadequacy by shutting down emotionally. I disengaged from the process. Like my shame-filled Eden parents before me, I hid. Shame led to withdrawal, which led to increased feelings of shame. Before I realized what was happening, I was caught in a downward shame spiral, with little hope for escape.[20]

Thankfully, God entered into my emotional collapse and lifted me up. Something in one of the sessions caused me to remember Mrs. Henshaw. The first Sunday school teacher I ever had, Mrs. Henshaw was a hard-of-hearing widow with white nose hairs so long and thick I'd sit in the back of the classroom and daydream about swinging from them. While other "cool" teachers brought in boom boxes with the latest DC Talk or other Christian hip-hop CD, Mrs. Henshaw lugged a portable record player from home and played old hymns or a Billy Graham sermon. (This was waaay before vinyl became all hipster and cool again. The revival of vinyl's coolness, by the way, makes me very happy because I have a pretty great record collection. Anyhow, back to the point.) There was nothing attractive, persuasive, or culturally savvy about Mrs. Henshaw. She was so boring even *she* would fall asleep in the middle of a lesson.

But here's the thing. Even though it's been twenty-five years since I walked into her classroom, I still remember Mrs. Henshaw and many of the lessons she taught. (How's that for effective leadership?) As I sat wallowing in shame at T-TAG, one lesson especially stood out: God's words to the prophet Samuel when he anointed a young shepherd named David to be Israel's future king.

Although David's older brothers were more impressive in stature and seemed to be the obvious candidates for leadership, God said to Samuel, "The LORD does not look at the things people look at. People look at the outward appearance, but the LORD looks at the heart" (1 Sam. 16:7).

It wasn't a new truth, but as I grappled with my insecurities and fears at T-TAG, God used Mrs. Henshaw's life, as well as her Bible lesson, to lift me out of my despair. Both Mrs. Henshaw and the future king of Israel were imperfect leaders, and yet God used each one powerfully, not in spite of their imperfections but through them.

Regardless of the form your shame might take, sooner or later it will try to make you feel disqualified so you question your ability to be a good *anything*—leader, employee, friend, date, spouse, parent, even child of God. But the truth for us today is the same truth that empowered Mrs. Henshaw and King

David. The grace of God is sufficient, not in spite of our weaknesses, brokenness, and shame but smack-dab in the middle of them. That's where the power is, according to the apostle Paul: "[The Lord] said to me, 'My grace is sufficient for you, for my power is made perfect in weakness.' . . . That is why, for Christ's sake, I delight in weaknesses. . . . For when I am weak, then I am strong" (2 Cor. 12:9–10).

Boom! I could not have said it better myself. If we believe we're insufficient (and even if in some circumstances we *are*), it doesn't even matter, because Jesus is more than sufficient and he qualifies us—for grace, for mercy, and for meaningful service in the kingdom of God.

From Shame to Radiance

Remember Psalm 34:5 from chapter 1? "Those who look to him are radiant; their faces are never covered with shame." One of the things I find most fascinating about this psalm is the context in which it was written, which includes some bewildering incidents about Mrs. Henshaw's David, recorded in 1 and 2 Samuel.

David is fleeing King Saul, who—threatened by David's success in battle and favor with God and the people—wants the charismatic young soldier dead. When David arrives at the city of Gath as a fugitive, he is recognized, arrested, and taken before Gath's king. In what is either an incredibly clever or an incredibly foolish move, David acts as if he's lost his mind: "So he pretended to be insane in their presence; and while he was in their hands he acted like a madman, making marks on the doors of the gate and letting saliva run down his beard" (1 Sam. 21:13).

Is this the image you typically associate with the ruddy and heroic shepherd boy who killed lions with his bare hands and braved the giant Goliath with just a slingshot? Yeah, me neither. I tend to think of David as a dauntless champion of the faith, always confident and brave. But this crazy act is not a courageous choice. We expect the heroic, giant-slaying David to rip off his shirt and boldly announce, "Yes! It is I!" while pummeling everyone around him. But that's not what happened. Instead, the text reveals that David "was very much afraid" of the king of Gath (1 Sam. 21:12). So much for his Marvel superhero status.

Now, let me remind you again, I grew up in the South. So this is the place in the Bible lesson where the Sunday school girl in me, wearing her frilly dress and white gloves, sipping sweet tea, and fanning herself on the porch, wants to shout, "David is lying! He's pretending to be something he's not! How is that okay, y'all?"

I like to think Mrs. Henshaw would have gently interrupted my shouting, complimented me on my fabulous gloves, and reminded me that David was terrified and running for his life. He'd lost everything—his family, his friends, his job, his status. As a prisoner of an enemy king, David was simply doing his creative best to protect himself. More significant, Mrs. Henshaw might have noted that David's actions are not what's most important about the events in 1 and 2 Samuel. She might even have gone so far as to say that David's story is not about David at all. It's about God's unwavering faithfulness in the midst of David's helplessness.

Falling for David's ruse, the king of Gath can't get rid of David fast enough: "Look at the man! He is insane! Why bring him to me? Am I so short of madmen that you have to bring this fellow here to carry on like this in front of me?" (1 Sam. 21:14). After his release, David finally finds sanctuary in the Cave of Adullam. And here's where the story gets downright amazing.

In the cave, God miraculously reunites David with his family! And then God appoints David leader over four hundred cave dwellers, people the Bible describes as being "in distress or in debt or discontented" (1 Sam. 22:2). This man, so recently acquainted with loss, pain, and defenselessness, becomes leader of a community covered in shame. This is the context in which David pens that beautiful promise: "Those who look to God are radiant; their faces are never covered with shame" (Ps. 34:5). Can you imagine how powerful it would have been for these people exiled by shame to hear their leader proclaim such words?

The truth in David's story—as well as in your story and mine—is that even when we are at our weakest, our most cowardly, our most shamed, God stands ready to intervene and redeem. He may do so in dramatic fashion, sweeping you away to a safe place to rest and recover. Or perhaps God will simply jog your memory so that a senior Sunday school teacher (with nose hairs the length of Victoria Falls) becomes a lifesaving reminder that God uses even the most unpolished of us to accomplish his will. Whatever redemption method he chooses, God's objective remains the same: to continually transform our shame into radiance and our misery into ministry.

Even if I wasn't the most polished leader at T-TAG, I figured if God could use Mrs. Henshaw's example decades later to minister to me, then I could at least try to climb out of my web of shame and give the assessment another shot. I may not have risen like a phoenix from the ashes (or received any MVP votes like Keviepoo—that show-off!), but by the end of the week, I was laughing with newfound friends, making memories with my husband, and seeking wisdom and feedback from the assessors. I finally understood that God didn't expect me to become perfect so that I would be eligible to plant a church. God would build his church and would use broken people (the only type there are) to do so. It was just a question of whether I would get on board and be a part of his amazing kingdom-building work.

When we returned home from boot camp, Kevin and I decided together it was time to launch Renewal Church. We've never looked back. (Our kids are raring to serve hot chocolate in the lobby this winter.)

Rahab, the Prostitute

Rahab was a prostitute in Jericho, an ancient city steeped in polytheistic culture. In a society and time when women were not highly esteemed, it's safe to assume her body, heart, and soul had been wounded in profound ways. This is not a woman we would expect God to use, but Rahab is praised throughout Scripture for her faith in God. When Joshua sent spies into Jericho, Rahab risked her life by hiding them from the king of Jericho. When the Israelites later conquered Jericho, Rahab and her family were saved. And even more amazing, Rahab became the great-great-grandmother of King David, and the great-great—to the twenty-eighth power or so—grandmother of Jesus. God not only renewed the heart of this former prostitute by empowering her with dignity and purpose; he placed her in Jesus' family tree!

Because Rahab's story is so triumphant and beautiful, it drives me absolutely batty when New Testament authors continue to refer to her as a prostitute:

- "By faith the prostitute Rahab, because she welcomed the spies, was not killed with those who were disobedient" (Heb. 11:31).

- "In the same way, was not even Rahab the prostitute considered righteous for what she did when she gave lodging to the spies and sent them off in a different direction?" (James 2:25).

I want her to be dubbed "Rahab the faithful" or "Rahab the transformed." She deserves a new title based on her faith and on the transformation God worked in her life. Even so, I've learned to make peace with it in the belief that overlooking Rahab's past would simply diminish the power of her beauty-from-ashes story. There is more redemptive power in her story because we know the full truth about her. In Rahab, we see how God's grace is available to all, no matter our upbringing, gender, ethnicity, or whatever we might consider shameful about our pasts. All we need to know about her is this: "Rahab the prostitute was considered righteous." That's the entire gospel summarized in six words.

It doesn't matter what has been done to us or what we've done to ourselves. There isn't anything beyond the reach of God's redemption. God loves to reveal his strength in our weaknesses. You can be used by God powerfully today, no matter what your yesterday looks like.

From Misery to Ministry

"If the gospel is renewing you internally, it will also be propelling you externally," write authors Robert Thune and Will Walker.[21] When you begin abiding in your Overcoming Shame Identity, there will be an outflow—a natural response to the transforming work God is doing in your life—that moves you outward. You'll be so changed by God's love that displaying that love to others will become as natural of an extension of you as your fingers and toes.

Shame may want us to believe our brokenness disqualifies us from being used by God. But just as David had more leadership influence because of what he'd been through, you have a contribution to make because of what you've been through. It is because you have battled, because you have scars, because you have suffered that you have something to offer. If you have known shame, and experienced freedom from it, there is no one better qualified than you to point others to that freedom.

Several years ago, we asked thousands of people from all across the world to pray for a very sick newborn child. We hoped with all our hearts that God would perform a miracle.

But when my best friend's curly headed baby boy died in her arms, she was launched into a season of incapacitating sorrow. God later blessed her and her husband with more beautiful children, and they have known joy since that awful day. But even so, there remains a dull and daily grief at the back of her throat, in the bottom of her heart, at the site of her C-section scar.

Jenn doesn't suffer from shame, necessarily, but her life has been a courageous demonstration of ministry born from misery. When others in our community, or even those on Facebook, suffer the loss of a child or have to care for sick babies, she is the first to pray for them and send a note of encouragement. On the other side of the token, as others around her give birth or adopt, she consistently showers the families with gifts and meals.

When my third son was born, not six months after hers died, Jenn visited me in the hospital and held my baby boy in the same room where she was forced to release hers. It was a painful irony, and yet she bore it with courage. Truly, Christ has been moving through her; that's the only way she could have displayed such powerful acts of love in the midst of her grief. She has given me a vivid picture of what it means to transform pain into purpose.

When you spend yourself on behalf of others, as the prophet Isaiah declared, "then your light will rise in the darkness, and your night will become like the noonday" (Isa. 58:10).

How can you live out your own version of light rising in the darkness or ministry from misery? Jenn poured herself out from one of the most vulnerable experiences of her life. How might you do the same? That question brings us back to our quiz.

Filling in the Blank Spaces (Remember the Quiz?)

Up to this point, we've focused on knocking down our Shame House while gently restoring the valuable, once-broken pieces. Now comes the fun part. As we begin to rebuild a new identity without shame, we get to decide what we want to do with all the empty space freed up by evicting our shame lies.

Demolishing Shame on Behalf of Others

As women who have been set free from shame, it is both our privilege and duty to go bashing down the doors of shame for those who can't do it themselves. In cases of global shames like human trafficking and slavery, there are a few practical ways you can begin helping others today.

Advocate. Call or tweet at your elected officials and tell them you are passionate about ending slavery and you'd like their support. Organizations such as International Justice Mission (IJM) or World Vision will sometimes provide sample letters and emails for communicating with your officials. You can also find your senators' contact information at the United States Senate website. (If you are nervous about calling your officials, there's no shame in dialing them up after hours and leaving a voicemail.) Just make sure your voice is heard!

Crowdsource. Grab some gal pals and meet regularly to pray for the estimated twenty-seven million victims of slavery around the world, for the one in four female victims of sexual assault, and for the one in seven male victims. You and your friends might also consider finding (or even forming) your own local anti-trafficking coalition. You can also go down to your local police station to discover what they're doing about trafficking in your town and how you and your group can assist.

Learn. The age we live in is an incredible one because we have access to so many informational resources. Websites like SlaveryFootprint.org and Free2Work.org can help you learn how your favorite brands and products relate to trafficking and labor abuses. You can also sign up for regular email updates from justice organizations such as IJM, End It Movement, the A21 Campaign, or World

Vision. Follow these groups on Twitter and your other social media venues. That way you'll stay informed of the latest and best practices for fighting against injustice.

Share. Use your social media accounts or the bulletin boards at local coffee shops to publicize the National Human Trafficking Resource Center hotline (NHTRC)—Call: 1-888-373-7888 or Text: HELP to BeFree (233733). The hotline is a confidential, around-the-clock, seven-days-a-week, toll-free number anyone can use to report a possible case of human trafficking or to request information and training.

Shop. Did you know that you can shop and simultaneously support organizations that help women all over the globe? It's true! The next time you need a gift, consider buying from organizations that are devoted to equipping and empowering women, such as International Sanctuary, Mudlove, Free the Girls, Made by Survivors, Christine Caine's A21 Campaign, and more. Shopping never felt so good!

Volunteer. For a time, I volunteered as a blogger for a former program of Women at Risk, International. I enjoyed using a familiar outlet (blogging) to send messages of love to victims. There are so many unique opportunities to empower women. From gathering and donating your friends' old bras to Free the Girls, to hosting parties through organizations like Trades of Hope, you can volunteer in small ways and make a big difference.

The quiz at the beginning of the chapter was not actually a quiz at all. (Insert shock and awe here!) It was designed to get you thinking about your passions and the things that are significant in your life. Why? Because these are the raw materials God uses to build something new in you, to transform your pain into purpose. As author Frederick Buechner writes, "the place God calls you to is the place where your deep gladness and the world's deep hunger meet."[22]

For those who have spent years shrouded in shame, it can be hard to believe God has designed you for something and designed something for you. But he has! When God set Adam and Eve to work in the garden, he wasn't just giving them some random way to while away their time. This was more than a job; he was providing them with a sense of purpose and vocational dignity—a calling.

With God, nothing is wasted. We tend to overthink things when it comes to identifying our God-given calling. I sometimes wish the term calling weren't even in our vocabularies, because we've morphed it into this confusing and mysterious thing, imagining some huge and scary task God wants us to do. Or we use calling as an excuse for inaction, as in, "Oh, sorry, that's not my calling, so I can't help you."

If we take a step back, identifying our place of influence in the world is pretty straightforward. God uses the things that have shaped our lives to help us care for others. That's our calling. "God designed and equipped each of us for the purpose of working through us to touch a lost and broken world," writes Bible teacher Christine Caine. "Basically our talents, passions, gifts, and interests are like a road map to discovering our unique life-print."[23] I'd also add your life's story to that list. God often uses the things we've been through to lead us into his calling for our lives.

Out of the pain of my experience on the bus and with my old boss came my passion to empower other women to experience freedom from shame in Christ, to live shamelessly. That's what I blog, write, and speak about. That calling was also formed through some other life experiences. For example, during my four years as a youth leader, I met a number of young women who were in the throes of eating disorders or suffering from low self-esteem. I wanted nothing more than to imprint upon them their identity as Christ's beloved daughters.

During the nine months Kevin and I served in Zambia, I had the heart-wrenching honor of sitting with women as they lay dying of HIV- and AIDS-related illnesses. I prayed for them and sang to them, but I could not do much in my short time there to ease their suffering or change their reality. God gave me a new sense of urgency to care for the dignity of other women and to support our Zambian friends who are still there ministering on a grassroots level. I also spent some time volunteering with Women at Risk, International (WAR, Int'l), a ministry dedicated to protecting at-risk women and children. And again, God used that experience to give me a passion to advocate for those who are unable to advocate for themselves.

I don't mean to say, "Oh, look at the amazing life lessons I learned from the suffering of others." (That would be gross.) But I *do* mean to say that God used each of these experiences to create a burden and a passion within me. He gave me the desire to see generations of women emotionally rise up, remove their ashes, heal from their pasts, and stand in Christ. And I want to see those women, in turn, begin ministering to others, creating a ripple effect of hope and healing.

A quick side note: I was an artsy little girl who would write poetry, mostly about roses and American birds, for some strange reason, and then ask the teacher if I could perform my poems for the class. (My poor fourth grade teacher. I'm sure she was like, "Oh, great, here comes Aubrey again with another brilliant piece on flamingos.") I've always enjoyed writing and public speaking. In giving me a calling, God combined my story (even the ugly parts) with my life experiences and added a dash of my interests. Just as he had for David, God turned what could have been a miserable shame story into a vocation.

If you're not already living out your calling, I'm sure you have an idea of what it might be. The cool thing is that you don't have to be in professional ministry to influence the world. You can live out your faith and be used by God right now, right where you are.

Maybe you refuse (most of the time) to give in to work gossip and instead, treat your coworkers with respect. Or you serve that especially frustrating person with integrity and patience. Perhaps you parent your tantruming toddler with grace (as much as you can muster). Maybe you're a thoughtful neighbor, in word and in deed. In these small but Christlike ways, your work, your volunteerism, and even your hobbies can be done in such a way that they provide you and those around you with a sense of dignity. A job is more than a job— it becomes a vocation—when it is done for the glory of God and the good of others.

If you're still wondering about and exploring your calling, take a look again at your responses to the quiz at the beginning of this chapter. As you review your answers, set aside time to go a little deeper by reflecting on the follow-up questions below. If you find it helpful, consider writing your responses in a notepad or journal as an additional means of reflection.

1. What do I wish, more than anything, to see God do through me?

2. What am I passionate about? What, if I did it, would make a real difference in my community or in the world?

3. If I could describe myself in ten years, what kind of woman do I hope to be? What do I want to be doing?

4. To what or whom would I dedicate my life?

5. If I had to determine one or two defining moments in life—things that have shaped me—what would I choose?

6. What are the big, even secret, dreams I've had since childhood?

7. How would I use my time and resources if they were unlimited?

After working through the reflection questions, ask God to help you recognize the ways in which he is already at work in your life. Continue praying for the ability to see what open doors might be right in front of you. Allow yourself to dream audaciously about how God might lead you into even more opportunities to use your life for the benefit of others.

Your story didn't end when shame began. God is still writing it. It is a story of grace and redemption, and it is far more beautiful than you can even imagine. Shame may try to disqualify you, like it did to me at T-TAG, but if God has called you to do something, he will give you all the radiance you need to shine.

DISCUSSION QUESTIONS

1. How do you tend to respond when you feel disqualified? Do you hide or withdraw, lash out against others, try to distract yourself? If you feel comfortable, share a recent example.

2. In what ways, if any, has shame led you to doubt yourself or your ability to make a difference for others?

3. What lessons have you learned from leaders in your life (past or present) about overcoming shame?

4. What do you find most meaningful about the stories of David or Rahab? Why?

5. Based on your responses to the quiz or your own experiences, how would you describe your calling—the ways in which God is transforming your pain into purpose, your misery into ministry?

6. If ministry begins right now, right where you are, how do you sense God may be inviting you to shine in and through your current situation?

PRAYER

God, I'm so thankful you're in control of my life and that you use imperfect people like David, Rahab, and me to do powerful things in your name. I want to be used by you to help someone else. Help me to see myself the way you see me and to believe you can transform my misery into ministry. Lift up my eyes and my heart to see the story you are writing through me. I love you. Amen.

AMY B.

Overcoming the Shame of an Abusive Marriage

"Dear Amy, you are no longer my wife," the typed page began. I stopped breathing. The letter contained accusations, insults, and threats about what would happen if I did not cooperate with my husband's plans to divorce me. To my shock, he also helped himself to our savings, cancelled credit cards, and moved in with another woman. While I hoped to wake from this terrible dream, divorce was my reality.

I never dreamed that my marriage would dump me into a wasteland at age thirty-two, or ever. Pain tore at me. My church upbringing had instilled in me the expectation that if a woman loves and serves a husband well enough, she will have a happy marriage and a happy life. I'd always envisioned starting a family in my thirties. Instead, I was moving from my cozy home into a rented room with a stranger I'd met through an ad. I was furious at how my former husband had destroyed my life. But shame continued to whisper its accusations: *If you were a better wife, your husband would love you. If you supported him better, sacrificed better, and loved better, then he would want to be with you. If you prayed more, with greater faith, God would change his heart and fix your marriage.*

A Christian therapist validated my hurt and anger. She also reminded me that there's a fine line between wanting justice and falling into bitterness. In a seminary class, I ran into a passage I'd always loved but somehow had forgotten: "He forgives your sins—every one. He heals your diseases—every one. He redeems you from hell—saves your life! He crowns you with love and mercy—a paradise crown. He wraps you in goodness—beauty eternal" (Ps. 103:3–5 MSG).

I felt ashamed of how ugly my resentment was making me. I kept wondering, *Am I any better for hating my former husband for the hateful things he's done to me?* I realized how much energy I was wasting obsessively rehashing his sins. While grieving was healthy, bitterness was ruining my life.

This line from the Lord's Prayer resonated with me: "Forgive us our debts, as we forgive those who are in debt to us." Knowing what forgiveness requires, I could not imagine letting my former husband off the hook. "No way!" I told God. "You shed your blood to make forgiveness possible. Doesn't letting him off without consequences cheapen your work on the cross?"

I yearned for freedom and eventually grew desperate enough to surrender to God my desire for justice. Although it was difficult at first, I started praying for my former husband. To be honest, those initial prayers were a little like throwing rocks at heaven. *I hate what he did, but please help him. Don't forget that he wrecked me, emotionally, socially, and financially, but please take care of him. Remember that he cheated on me, but give him wisdom in his next relationship.*

With time, I felt a measure of earnestness weave its way into my prayers for him. It wasn't instantaneous. I still tossed raw prayers toward heaven and half expected God to respond to me with divine anger or at least disappointment. Surprisingly, though, God wrapped me in exquisite love. Eventually, the chains binding me to shameful hurt, anger, and desire for revenge disintegrated. It took many, many years, but I found increasing freedom as I continued to pray and as the Holy Spirit cultivated a heart of forgiveness.

I found a new energy and focus as I learned that God never entitles one partner to live selfishly at the expense of the other. My former husband sinned when he neglected our relationship and bullied me to get his way. I learned that being a helper doesn't entail sacrificing everything to the detriment of God's purposes. When in dire straits, the Israelites called upon God as their strong help. I learned that women are uniquely created to strengthen their community, and that became my calling.

I was invited to work as a teaching assistant at the seminary I attended. I traveled to conferences to promote peace and safety in the home. Since graduating with a masters of divinity, I've advocated for both men and women as I write and speak about bringing Christ's presence to those suffering domestic and sexual violence. And I'm getting better at putting on my spiritual armor and trusting Jesus to tell off the devil and the shame he rode in on.

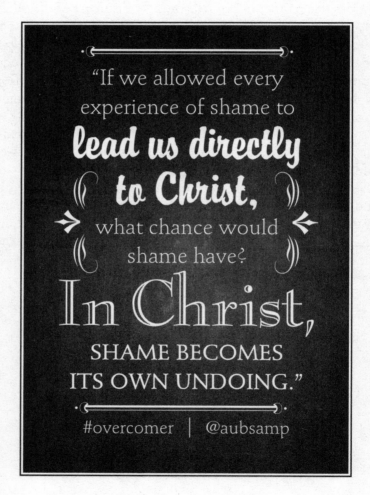

"If we allowed every experience of shame to **lead us directly to Christ,** what chance would shame have? In Christ, SHAME BECOMES ITS OWN UNDOING."

#overcomer | @aubsamp

Chapter 7

FOR THE DAYS YOU LOSE IT IN PUBLIC

Facing Commonplace Shame

SHAME'S LIE: SHAME IS EXPERIENCED
ONLY IN TRAUMATIC SITUATIONS.

OVERCOMER'S TRUTH: SHAME
IS IN THE MUNDANE, AND THERE
IS A BRIGHT SIDE TO IT.

You know *that* mom at the grocery store? The one we all promise ourselves we're never going to turn into? The lady yelling at her kids, causing a scene, and basically saying farewell to every last shred of cool she may have had. I'm not talking about the cute mom in kitten heels and 7 for All Mankind jeans. No, this is the lady in jeggings, no makeup, and a sloppy ponytail.

Recently—and I hate to admit it, because I know my reputation as a fashionista/trendsetter/chic mama is on the line—I became that woman. I don't have a good reason. It was just one of those days. I mean, I might as well have gone to the grocery store wearing a terry cloth robe and velcro rollers. (I *was* donning yoga pants and a Mickey Mouse sweatshirt, so not much of an improvement.)

I spent most of the trip ~~flinging food~~ gently placing our healthy, nutrient-rich provisions into the cart, while ~~yelling at~~ patiently encouraging my three sons to ~~"Sit still and stop eating all the groceries before we even leave the store!"~~ "Practice gentlemanly patience until we can consume our daily bread in the privacy of our own home."

I pulled into the checkout line sweaty from stress and exhaustion. The phrases "hot mess" and "she's got issues" come to mind. The checkout lady must have been having a day of her own. She took one glance at our melee and decided this was an opportune moment to step onto a soapbox. No, not a soapbox . . . a stage. In a voice loud enough for the customers on the other side of the store to hear, she reprimanded me because my four-year-old wasn't properly buckled into the cart.

I know what you're thinking, and let me just stop you right there. Yes, he should've been securely fastened. Yes, I was letting things go. I own it. But for the record, the kid was keeping himself entertained by buckling and unbuckling the seat belt . . . for the entire shopping trip! Enough said. Maybe you don't have kids, or maybe you *are* the cute mom at the store (#ihateyoualittlebit), but let's just imagine for a moment that one day you find yourself at the grocery store in Disney-inspired sweats, attempting to manage a shopping list, a budget, three kids, and your dignity; and on that same day, one of those three kids is miraculously keeping himself occupied with a plastic buckle. I have a feeling you too will let the seat belt slide. (If I'm wrong, just never ever tell me, please.) Permit me to walk you through our little nine-part grocery-store melodrama.

PART 1: *The Moment in Which, after Being Reprimanded Publicly, I Attempt to Keep Things Light*

ME: I know. He should absolutely be wearing his seat belt. He keeps taking the silly thing off then buckling it again. He's having so much fun. What can you do?

Crazy kids. (Here, I inserted a little giggle I hoped would communicate, *Be cool, lady*.)

PART 2: *The Moment in Which, Shockingly, the Cashier Does Not Respond to Subtext of Giggle (and Also Refers to Me as "Ma'am")*

HER: Ma'am, I understand your predicament, but store policy states I cannot load your groceries unless your son puts on his seat belt.

PART 3: *The Moment in Which I Endeavor to Appeal to the Cashier's Sensitive Side*

ME: Look, I'm just trying to survive this outing. Can you please help a mom out? Woman to woman, I'm doing the best I can here.

PART 4: *The Moment in Which the Cashier Does. Not. Budge.*

HER: Ma'am, you need to take your child out of the cart or buckle him in; otherwise, I won't be able to give you your items.

PART 5: *The Moment in Which I Begin to Lose It*

ME: You're seriously telling me if I don't force my four-year-old son to keep his seat belt buckled, you won't give me my food?

PART 6: *The Moment in Which the Cashier Does. Not. Budge. Again. (And, by the Way, Calls Me Ma'am a Third Time. Enough Already with the Ma'am!)*

HER: Yes, ma'am. That's store policy.

PART 7: *The Most Mature Moment of My Existence*

ME: This is the most ridiculous thing I have ever dealt with! (I yelled this statement, by the way. Not a whisper, not even a raised voice. This was a full-on, causing-even-more-people-to-stare-at-me, yell.) I then proceeded to yank my child out of the grocery cart with such pomp and circumstance that I just knew the cashier would have to recognize the error of her ways. The customers in line behind me would applaud. The manager would come over and offer her sincerest apologies. My righteous indignation, in light of this unjust personal affront, would be rewarded with a lifetime supply of gift cards.

PART 8: *The Moment in Which My Son Makes His Feelings Known*

MY SON: *(crying)*

PART 9: *The Moment in Which the Cashier Revels in Her Triumph*

HER: Now, then. Would you like paper or plastic? (Here she inserted her own giggle, which I can only assume was designed to communicate, *I win. I win. Ha ha ha. That's right. I called you ma'am. I'll do it again . . . ma'am.*)

Aaaaand . . . scene.

I stomped out of the store, huffing and puffing the entire way. I hurled my kids and groceries into the car and clambered into the driver's seat, where I stopped for a beat and tried unsuccessfully to pull myself together. Leaning my forehead against the hot leather steering wheel, I prayed the heat would burn away my tears. I was embarrassed by the way the cashier had called me out publicly, and I was mortified by my immature reaction. She may have set the shame stage, but I assumed the role: naked, center spotlight, shame shrieking like the feedback off a poorly positioned microphone.

The Minor Scenes of Shame—and Grace

Shame isn't always a thug from the past, crouching in a dark corner waiting to sucker punch you in the gut. Sometimes shame is more like a ballerina, deftly dancing through the mundane and taking an unanticipated swipe at you as she glides by. Which is why we need to address lie number six in the Shame House: *shame is experienced only in traumatic situations.*

That day at the grocery store may have been a minor scene on the stage of life, but that's exactly my point. Shame *is* at the grocery store when you least expect it, when you're praying no one sees you in your sweatpants because you didn't have the emotional wherewithal to get dressed that day. Shame is in the checkout line, when your child won't stay buckled in or your meager budget doesn't allow for the brand-name products you wish you were purchasing.

We tend to associate feeling ashamed with the dark and heavy secrets of our past, but shame can also be unassuming. There's living room shame, when you laugh uncomfortably and apologize to your guests because your condo isn't sparkling clean. We're all familiar with bathroom shame, when the reflection in the mirror showcases belly fat, when stepping onto the scale might break you, when you're crying alone in the shower. Shame sips a latte in the coffee house, sneaks up on you at the gym, and slides up next to you at school or work. But just because shame can strike in mundane situations does not mean it's any less painful or overwhelming.

That day in the grocery store, I was the poster child for shame in the mundane, a living portrait of the Shamed Woman. Keep that image in mind, because I want to paint another scene, also mundane, but this time, instead of shame, it is a picture of grace.

The Sunday after Seat Belt Gate, still reeling from anger and embarrassment, I took a seat in the back of the church, praying that no one there had witnessed my tantrum at the store. I sat behind an elderly couple whom I recognized but didn't know. The wife wore her lovely white hair in a long braid down her back, the tail of which brushed against what appeared to be an elastic strap of some kind. Her husband sported a pair of trendy suspenders. They were, altogether, a very cool looking couple (and definitely not the type of people who lost that cool in public).

That morning, the preacher, who also happens to be my husband, so I will say only wonderful things about his sermon, spoke about being thankful in all circumstances. "Not," he clarified, "*for* all circumstances—there is evil and darkness in this world we will never be thankful for—but *in* all circumstances."

Was I thankful in that scene at the store? Could I ever learn to be thankful in such moments? Kevin ended his message by reminding us that Jesus doesn't come into our lives with cliches. He did not walk on this earth to make the glass half full or to teach us to look at the silver lining in life. The Son of God does not invite his followers into a life of platitudes. No, instead he changes our paradigm. He renews all things, including us.

You've probably heard some version of the saying, "God accepts us fully as we are, but that doesn't mean he wants to keep us there." I sat in church sensing that God wanted to use my grocery store melodrama—that mundane moment of shame—to do something new in me. But what, exactly?

When the congregation stood for the closing song, the elderly woman in front of me remained in her seat, but she lifted her hands and sang. And by sang I mean she *saaaang*. She belted out those worship songs like she was auditioning for some reality TV singing competition. After a few verses, her arms started to shake from fatigue. I expected her to put her hands down. Instead, she did something unexpected.

She tapped her husband on the back. He recognized his cue, grabbed the strap around her waist and gently pulled his wife to a standing position. She leaned on him with one arm and lifted the other in an almost defiant act of praise. Nothing would keep her from worshiping Jesus. If it was possible, she sang now with even more power. With the passion of Aretha, Adele, and Mandisa all rolled into one.

Then it hit me. *Here she is*, I thought. *The antithesis of me at the grocery store; this woman is a living portrait of Overcoming.* It was a simple moment really. There is nothing incredibly profound about a woman singing at church. I mean, there are millions of them in churches all over the world every week. If she had given up, if she had just sat down, I probably wouldn't have even noticed; that would have been the expected choice. But she did the unexpected thing, and it took me by surprise. She refused to allow her circumstances to dictate her attitude. She rose. She worshiped. She overcame.

And although this woman wasn't dealing with shame, per se, her determination—her nothing-will-get-me-down attitude—inspired me. I could have done the unexpected thing at the store. I could have showed the cashier some patience. I could have responded with dignity. I could have set a better example for my children. I could have risen above the drama, rather than playing a part in it. (I considered causing even more drama by inciting a social media riot that would result in the closing of the entire franchise. Not that it would have worked, but it is fun to imagine I have that much power.)

And okay, so maybe the cashier wasn't the bright and shining pinnacle of customer service, but frankly, it wasn't up to me to change her role in the conflict. I could do something only about myself. Sitting in church that morning, after hearing the sermon (by that ever so cute and talented pastor), and after watching the Overcoming Woman fight to worship, I knew I needed to return to the store. I needed to redeem that moment by showing the cashier the grace of God. I only hoped that by doing so, I'd experience more of it myself and bring the curtain down on shame.

Shame Doesn't Have to Be a Scene Stealer

Believe it or not, there is a bright side to shame. Shame can be a prison guard, but it can also hand you the keys to freedom. It can paralyze or motivate you.[24] Let's be honest; if our shame is hitting the fan, we tend to justify it, ignore it, or allow it to consume us. But if we stop long enough to reflect on our shame, it can become like a signal indicating a need for change,

Toxic Shame versus the Holy Spirit

Toxic shame is a weapon used by Satan to condemn, control, and incarcerate. In absolute contrast, the Holy Spirit's work in your life leads to repentance, forgiveness, and liberation. May these truths from Romans 8 remind you of the power of the Spirit of God in your life and enable you to live in freedom from mundane shame.

The Holy Spirit:

- *resides in you.* "You, however, are not in the realm of the flesh but are in the realm of the Spirit, if indeed the Spirit of God lives in you. And if anyone does not have the Spirit of Christ, they do not belong to Christ" (Rom. 8:9).

- *releases you from captivity to fear.* "The Spirit you received does not make you slaves, so that you live in fear again" (Rom. 8:15a).

- *reminds you God is your loving Father.* "You received God's Spirit when he adopted you as his own children" (Rom. 8:15b NLT).

- *reassures you of your future with God.* "Now if we are children, then we are heirs—heirs of God and co-heirs with Christ, if indeed we share in his sufferings in order that we may also share in his glory" (Rom. 8:17).

- *requests God's help on your behalf.* (That's a simple way of saying the Holy Spirit prays for you. I just really liked how the *r* verbs were rolling out.) "In the same way, the Spirit helps us in our weakness. We do not know what we ought to pray for, but the Spirit himself intercedes for us through wordless groans" (Rom. 8:26).

humility, or spiritual growth. If we let him, God can use our mundane experiences of shame as occasions for grace. This means every shame experience has the potential to be a sign-post that reminds us of our need for a Savior. Think about it. If we allowed every experience of shame to lead us directly to Christ, what chance would shame have? In Christ, shame becomes its own undoing.

We're all big kids. This isn't a new life lesson. But it's still one worth remembering. When you're the one who does something unkind or careless, when you're the one who's act-ed shamefully, in order to grow in maturity, you have to put on your big girl pants, humble yourself, admit your fault, and apologize. Otherwise, you'll just end up spreading your shame around and sitting in it. And trust me, because I've changed a lot of diapers, no one likes to sit around in their own mess.

We might contribute to shame. We might even *be* the shamers ourselves. But if we can own our responsibility and our sinfulness, then shame does not have to own us. God-ly sorrow, which leads to repentance and spiritual growth, is a good thing. Shame, on the other hand, leads only to con-demnation and incarceration. However, when we bring even mundane experiences of shame to God, he invades and illumi-nates them with his extraordinary grace. They are, as we are, redeemed.

When I returned to the store (this time I left the kiddos at home), I was secretly hoping to avoid actual human interac-tion and leave the cashier a note of apology. As providence would have it, this was her shift.

"I don't know if you remember me," I said sheepishly, "but I owe you an apology for my attitude the other day."

I wish I could tell you it ended like a scene from a Holly-wood movie: we hugged and laughed uproariously about the whole to-do. Now we wear matching BFF necklaces and meet for coffee and pedicures every Saturday, and I even dedicated this book to her. Mostly, she didn't remember me, which also goes to show shame's bad habit of making things a bigger deal in our minds than they actually are. In the end, she thanked me for returning, told me no one had ever done that before, and we giggled together (albeit a bit awkwardly).

Shame Triggers

There's another bright side to shame in these day-to-day melodramas. Mundane moments of shame can provide opportunities for self-reflection and emotional growth. People often say that shame is about who you are; guilt is about what you do. That can be a helpful differentiation, but it is a bit of an oversimplification. Sometimes the things we do are triggered by our shame. When you catch yourself responding to a situation or to a loved one with an overreaction—an anger or sadness that perhaps was a little larger than the situation warranted—those moments are called shame triggers. You might be fuming mad or miserably depressed, but what's underneath those emotions could actually be shame. Stop long enough to think about what triggered your big reaction. Ask yourself questions like, "When have I felt this before? Did I feel this as a child? Is this familiar to me?" This will most likely lead to an emotional discovery which God can use to heal, sanctify, change, and renew you.

As I reflected on and assessed my beastly actions at the grocery store, yes, I was embarrassed about how I looked. I was flustered because my kids weren't on their best Boy Scout behavior. And my tantrum? Super sophisticated. Underneath it all, though, I didn't even care about being reprimanded for the seat belt. When we feel in danger of failing or being found out as failures, we are so much more likely to react strongly to others. The cashier called me out about the seat belt and unknowingly unearthed a hidden fear, which, in turn, triggered my shame.

I entered the grocery store that day at the end of a pay period. Concerned about the limited amount of food I was able to purchase for my family, I was anxiety-ridden about how I was going to creatively stretch the food dollars we had until our next payday. Before the cashier said one word, I was already steeping in a toxic brew of shame: *I wouldn't be in this situation if I could manage our budget better. What will I do if I can't keep these three hungry boys fed? My parents always provided financially for me as a kid. What kind of mother am I?*

The shame I experienced that day wasn't caused by the seat belt confrontation alone. It was a conglomeration of financial shame, bad-mommy shame, appearance shame, and failure shame. Nothing in the situation was life altering or painfully traumatic, but shame was nonetheless rearing its ugly head. When I stopped long enough to realize what was truly triggering my shame, God used that knowledge to lop it off.

I am your provider. He reminded me. *You are my daughter. I have always taken care of you and your family and always will.* God took me back to a place, emotionally, where I could receive his love, and in that way, shame was forced to make a final exit.

There will likely be more embarrassing scenes in public (or, if you're less like me and more like a normal person, these will happen in the privacy of your own home). If we can remember that God uses our mundane moments of shame as opportunities to display his grace and mercy, then we can experience the bright side of shame. Let's just all hope we have on a cute pair of jeans the next time it happens.

DISCUSSION QUESTIONS

1. When are you most likely to experience shame in a mundane situation? If you feel comfortable, share a recent example.

2. How do you respond to the idea that there is a bright side to shame? In what ways, if any, would you say you've experienced the bright side of shame?

3. Think about a moment when you've been the shamer or you've acted shamefully. How did you feel afterward? If you could redo that moment, what would you do differently?

4. What inspires or encourages you to face and overcome your mistakes?

5. Think about a recent time you had a strong emotional reaction. What triggered that response? What, if anything, was underneath your emotion? What might God want to show you, or develop in you, through that situation?

PRAYER

Dear God, sometimes I am a big old mess. I'm so thankful I don't have to try to be otherwise in front of you because you know me so well and you see all of me. When I experience shame in my daily life, would you help me learn and grow from it? If I've acted shamefully or sinfully, would you help me quickly make corrections, not because I'm trying to be perfect but because I want to overcome shame. I need your help to do all these things. I worship you, God, because you are so powerful and good that even shame cannot remain as shame in you. Thank you for loving me. Amen.

AMY N.

Overcoming the Shame of High Standards

I have a confession to make: I am not a good enough friend.

The moment will always be engrained in my memory. It was nearing midnight, and my housemate "Amber" sat on our couch, snotty-nosed and puffy-eyed, her white V-neck tee soaked with a salty combination of sweat and tears. I took a deep breath as I plopped down beside her and placed my hand on her back. As I looked into her hazel eyes, I knew that although she was a sensitive person, this was not the usual drama. Tonight was different. My friend's life was quickly falling apart. I watched as the pieces of who she was and who she wanted to be crashed to the floor. The truths she spoke, and the many I heard in the silences between sobs, scared me.

Then came the pressure. The weight of carrying another's burdens. The anxiety that kept me up all night. The desire to say the exact right words at the exact right time to convey all the love I wanted Amber to hear. The heaviness of wanting to fix things for her. The wishing I could change her situation and help her see a brighter tomorrow. The deep longing I had to heal her. The selfish thought that maybe I could and should control the chaos so that her questions and emotions didn't have to make me feel uncomfortable anymore.

I desperately wanted to be a good friend, the best friend I could possibly be for Amber's sake. But living up to the standards in my mind was impossible.

I am not a good enough friend.

This was not the first time I felt the shame of not being able to give others what I thought they deserved or needed or expected. It was not the last time I felt the shame of missing the mark I'd set for myself. This was the ordinary shame I felt quite regularly.

I wanted to be a good friend, but as I sat listening to Amber spill out her sorrows and sins, I had no idea what to do. I should have prayed for her out loud then, but I didn't. I should have said more kind words than I did or hugged her longer or . . . something, anything.

In the days and months that followed, I tried my best to navigate my relationship with Amber, all the while feeling frustrated that I couldn't give her everything she needed. I wasn't God. I was human. And as much as I wanted to be there for her, my love wasn't perfect, and my friendship had limits.

For the next year, as I watched Amber struggle to make wise decisions, I wrestled with the guilt that I wasn't a good enough friend. Daily, I felt it, not only with Amber but with others too. When someone needed advice, I couldn't always give it. When someone wanted encouraging words, sometimes I couldn't think of any. When someone asked for a gentle touch, sometimes I wasn't in the mood. When someone hoped I'd be free, sometimes I didn't have the time.

Then one day Amber and I sat down to chat over coffee. Conversations had been rough recently, and I wasn't really looking forward to having this one. Amber had insisted that we meet though. So I went, not really knowing what to expect but anticipating difficulties. She still wasn't doing that great.

We talked for a while. I was trying my best to love her well, but I felt like I wasn't doing a good job. Finally, I voiced this frustration, and she said something I needed to hear:

"Amy, you are never going to be good enough." Amber paused and looked at me with grace glimmering in her eyes. "But I hope you know that you *are* enough."

The weight I'd been carrying for so long was suddenly lifted. Believing those few words was the key to freedom from my shame. Amber was right. I wasn't ever going to be a good enough friend to her or to anyone else. I couldn't live up to the lofty standards I wanted to follow. While the Bible called me to love others, it also said that love is a fruit of the Spirit. God is love, and out of that truth, I had hope to love others too. It was not through my own strength or power, but through his. He makes me enough.

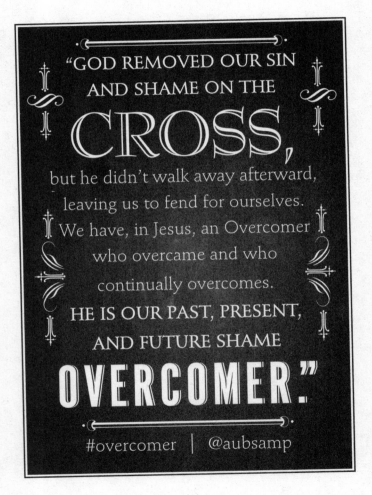

"GOD REMOVED OUR SIN AND SHAME ON THE **CROSS,** but he didn't walk away afterward, leaving us to fend for ourselves. We have, in Jesus, an Overcomer who overcame and who continually overcomes. HE IS OUR PAST, PRESENT, AND FUTURE SHAME **OVERCOMER."**

#overcomer | @aubsamp

Chapter 8

FINISHING TOUCHES

The Ongoing Adventure of Overcoming Shame

Kevin and I went to Disney World on our honeymoon. (Before you judge us, we also spent part of our honeymoon at a romantic resort in Mexico.) As you have been made aware of at this point, I wave my Disney World freak flag proudly, so I made Kevin escort me as his new bride to "The Happiest Place on Earth." While we were there, I also made him wear T-shirts that matched mine. I thought it'd be sort of ironic and hilarious to look like a "typical honeymooning couple." As it turns out, when you're actually on your honeymoon, it's not all that ironic; we just looked cheesy. The honeymoon pictures of us in our matchy-matchy outfits still crack me up, though, so it was worth it.

One day during our vacation, we ventured out to a bookstore in Orlando and began browsing the store's CD selection. (For those of you who were born in the '90s, CDs are magical round discs that contain music. You place one into a large electronic box called a CD player and then listen as sounds and melodies come out of it . . . and while we're at it, a bookstore is a wonderful place filled with rectangular-shaped items made from paper and words.)

Anyway, this girl, maybe fifteen or sixteen years old, came up to us and asked what music we were into. Then she just started talking on and on about a friend she used to go to high school with who had a new CD out, and how this friend was on the brink of stardom, and had we heard of her, because if not, we soon would. After she finished chatting with us, I watched her approach other shoppers and do the same thing to them, shoving into their faces a CD with her friend's image on the cover. (In case you're dying of curiosity, this little starlet went on to become singer and actress Mandy Moore, the voice of Rapunzel from Disney's *Tangled*, I might add.)

This girl was so ecstatic just to be celebrity-adjacent. I remember thinking it was cool how excited she was for her newly famous friend, but also feeling sad for her. I wondered if she'd spend her entire existence in that bookstore, telling people about her friend's stardom while never shining in her own life.

You can sit in front of whoever will listen and tell them how much you desperately want to be free from shame. You can stand unashamed-adjacent. Or you can start living your life as the overcomer you were meant to be. If I haven't been clear by now, let me state it again: Jesus died and rose again, once and for all, so that you can be free from the power and penalty of sin and shame. And he, who began that good work in you, will carry it on to completion (Phil. 1:6). Jesus removed our sin and shame on the cross, but he didn't walk away afterward, leaving us to fend for ourselves. We have, in Jesus, an Overcomer who overcame and who continually overcomes. He is our past, present, and future shame Overcomer.

Now it's time for us to start living like it.

The final lie residing in our Shame House is this: *The goal of overcoming shame is never to encounter it again.* The goal of overcoming shame isn't to arrive at some fairy-tale destination, where you've learned your lesson and now you live in a guarded castle and never have to deal with the dragon of shame again. The goal is to continue overcoming shame as long as you walk on God's green earth. Don't let that statement defeat you—shame does not have to be your identity. It will shrink from a huge fire-breathing serpent into a small annoying bug. But just as a bee can be dead and still have a sting, shame has been destroyed in Christ, but the remains can be irritating. True victory over shame is in the willingness to continue fighting against it.

For a time, I went back and forth about a name for "The Overcoming Shame Identity" (which you're about to see unveiled in chapter 9). I thought about calling it "The Unashamed Identity," "The Free from Shame Identity," or even "The Shameless Identity." I ended up sticking with "The Overcoming Shame Identity" because I like the way the verb overcoming signals an action. We, who are overcoming shame, are participating in an ongoing adventure.

Maybe you're already experiencing some amazing results of freedom from shame in Christ. You believe in and love yourself again, or for the first time. You've forgiven yourself for your mistakes. Your relationships are healthier. You have finally stopped hiding and have allowed others to see the real you. You're experiencing God's love in new ways. You're pouring your life out for others. If that's you, I'm so thankful!

For those of you who are still in the thick of fighting against shame, or for those of you just wanting a few more action steps, I wanted to equip you with six overcoming-shame tools—weapons to assist in the adventure of slaying the dang thing.

Overcoming Shame: Six Weapons

1. Continue to Acknowledge Shame

I know that sounds like a strange weapon. This whole book has been about overcoming shame. Why would I want you to keep acknowledging it? Because learning to continually recognize our shame, when it happens, is a step in the process of releasing it. Marriage and family therapist Dr. John Amodeo offers helpful guidance about how to recognize and overcome shame in the moment: "If you try to strong-arm yourself into getting rid of your shame or think something's wrong with you for having it, you'll only intensify it. A step toward healing shame is to notice when it arises. How does it feel in your body? Meeting it with kindness and curiosity allows you to find some distance from it. A step toward greater freedom is learning to have a relationship with shame rather than being fused with it."[25]

Anytime you feel ashamed, instead of running away from the emotion, give yourself permission to pause and simply pay attention to it. Approach shame like it's your crazy old uncle, carefully, but with genuine curiosity about why he's out in public again. "Hey, Shame, I notice you are back. Why are you here again? What has triggered your return?"

It sounds counterintuitive. When we feel this way, we generally don't want to invite shame in for dinner and a nightcap. But a gentle and welcoming approach to shame can go a long way toward eventually closing the door even tighter on it. As we learn to recognize the moments or patterns or people that trigger our shame, we can continually equip ourselves to overcome it.

2. Regularly Remind Yourself of God's Truth

Shame may be loud, but God's Word is always louder. As I've been writing this book, there have been moments when the process has dredged up shameful memories. I've spent many mornings reminding myself of these words: "I am he who will sustain you. I have made you and I will carry you; I will sustain you and I will rescue you" (Isa. 46:4).

Just reading that verse aloud and reminding myself of the truth from God's Word has empowered me as I continue my own overcoming-shame training. Go back to God's Word again and again, because his truth is able to conquer any of the lies shame throws your way. The following list contains some of my favorite Scriptures on overcoming shame. May they speak to you as powerfully as they have spoken to me.

Reference	Scripture	I Praise You, Jesus, Because . . .
Genesis 2:25	"Adam and his wife were both naked, and they felt no shame."	You are the creator of all, and you designed me to live without shame.
Psalm 25:3	"No one who hopes in you will ever be put to shame, but shame will come on those who are treacherous without cause."	When I put my hope in you, I am never left feeling ashamed. You do not ignore those who take advantage of others.
Psalm 34:5	"Those who look to him are radiant; their faces are never covered with shame."	You change my shame to beaming, radiant joy.
Isaiah 54:4	"Do not be afraid; you will not be put to shame. Do not fear disgrace; you will not be humiliated. You will forget the shame of your youth and remember no more the reproach of your widowhood."	In you, I do not fear shame or disgrace. You remove the shame from my life.
Romans 10:11	"As the Scripture [Isa. 28:16] says, 'Anyone who believes in [Jesus] will never be put to shame.'"	I trust in you, and because of that, I will never be put to shame.
1 Corinthians 1:27	"But God chose the foolish things of the world to shame the wise; God chose the weak things of the world to shame the strong."	You use the most unexpected of us to do your will. You can even use me.

Hebrews 12:1–2	"And let us run with perseverance the race marked out for us, fixing our eyes on Jesus, the pioneer and perfecter of faith. For the joy set before him he endured the cross, scorning its shame, and sat down at the right hand of the throne of God."	You overcame shame forever on the cross. You endured the ultimate shame so that I no longer have to. When you overcame shame, you took your rightful place at the right hand of God. You are King over everything, including my circumstances and my past.
1 Peter 2:6	"For in Scripture [Isa. 28:16] it says: 'See, I lay a stone in Zion, a chosen and precious cornerstone, and the one who trusts in him will never be put to shame.'"	You are the precious and chosen cornerstone, the rock on which I stand. I will put my trust in you and will never be put to shame. You are worthy to receive praise.

3. Enjoy the Little Things

One of my closest friends is a total fashionista. She shops well and generously shares items she no longer wears. I have been the blessed recipient of many of her chic boutique hand-me-downs. Once, at a girls night out, she (being the love child of Mary Poppins and Santa Claus that she is) brought in three huge garbage bags full of dresses, tops, and cute shoes for a few of us to sort through. We all shrieked in delight. I grabbed a pair of boots, a skirt, and even a few accessories.

Everything was fine and dandy and sparkly until out came The Sweater. A flattering cut. A beautiful color. Cashmere. And my size. When another woman, someone I did not know well, grabbed the sweater of the gods before I had a chance to, I entertained what I considered at the time to be some completely reasonable and levelheaded thoughts, such as, *Why should* she *get the sweater?* And, *That's* my *sweater!* I may have even pulled out the pastor-martyr card: *We're in ministry. Doesn't she understand we are basically forced to wait on God for every one of our needs?*

And I neeeeeeeed that sweater. I practically had to stop myself from ripping the sweater out of her greedy little hands.

I played it totally cool on the outside, but on the inside, I was a ball of cray cray. (Yes, cray cray is the scientific term for what was happening in my soul.) Then I had this sort of out-of-body experience in which I watched myself becoming a gold digger of a woman, suddenly possessed by greed and materialism. Just a few seconds earlier, I had been delighted, squealing girlishly about my new boots. But now, in light of what I didn't have, my treasures were no longer enough. I also realized I was actually thinking of another sister in Christ as a person with "greedy little hands."

Whether it's a Facebook status, a financial situation, a degree, a career, a relationship, a Pinterest kitchen, a body type, or a stupid sweater, when we focus on things others have—things that we want—we can begin to feel ashamed either for not having them or for becoming total greed monsters for wanting them.

Allow me to reassure you that I'm not asking you to fake an emotion or to thank God for anything evil or tragic in your life. I'm inviting you instead to fight shame with an action—a simple thank you. Punch shame in the nuts by making it a daily habit to thank God for the good you can identify, however small. You'll find yourself moving away from complaining about everything you don't have, toward worshiping God for his provision of everything you need.

4. Stop "Shoulding" All Over Yourself

If "shoulding" were a sport, I'd be a contender for MVP. And the capacity in which I'd win is in my role as a pastor's wife. The weird thing is I don't think anyone actually has the expectations I imagine they do. But sometimes I invent requirements for my role as a pastor's wife based on what I wrongly perceive are other people's standards for me. It's exhausting. One way I do this is by putting pressure on myself to be some amazing old-school hostess who invites people over for tea trays and

It's the Little Things

I once challenged a group of women to inventory their favorite little joys in life. Here is their inspiring list:

> The smell of freshly brewed coffee
> Birds chirping
> A baby's laughter
> Watching a pet get excited over a toy or treat
> An unexpected phone call or text from a friend
> A stranger opening the door for you or letting you merge in traffic
> A surprise kiss from a loved one
> Naps
> Receiving a compliment
> Helping out someone when they are swamped at work
> Taking a walk outside
> Watching children play
> Sleeping with the windows open
> Relaxing with family or friends on the porch after a long day
> The smell of freshly cut grass in the spring
> Lazy winter Sundays on the couch, with movies, blankets, and delicious snacks
> The scent of burning leaves in the fall
> Watching kids discover something new for the first time
> Discovering that you and the person next to you at a stoplight are listening to the same song on the radio
> Laughing so hard you can't breathe
> Summertime at dusk

A stranger anonymously paying for your meal

Free concerts in the city

Sunsets at the beach

Stars

Singing in the car with friends

The taste of batter before you bake cookies, brownies, or cake

Reconnecting with old friends as if no time has passed

Love notes

Holding hands

Having your hair washed at the salon

Seeing newlyweds take pictures after their ceremony

crumpets and finger sandwiches. (Frankly, I don't know if any of those are even real things.)

Maybe you feel similarly, like you should fit into some stereotypical mold of the perfect Christian gal. She listens only to Christian radio. She never swears. She lives by strict rules. She's a good person all the time. She never messes up. Or perhaps you have a high need to be the perfect mom who never entertains her children with screen time and transforms every mundane experience into a life lesson. (Don't eat the Legos, Timmy. If you can get that, you'll go far in life.)

We *all* put expectations on ourselves to be achievers—women who are physically, financially, stylistically, emotionally, and spiritually successful. When we're unable to bear up under the pressure of all this "shoulding," it slams back down on us and shame bursts out.

If Jesus doesn't "should" on us—if he doesn't pressure us to be someone we're not—why do we constantly do it to ourselves? My friend Jess said it best: "People think they should live by all these rules, and if they don't, then they aren't a

Christian. I try to live my life the way God planned for me. I try to put him first in everything and turn to him. Do I do that all the time? No. But that's what being a Christian is: accepting that you are not perfect, but the Lord is, and he accepts you even when you are in your worst state and helps you become more like him along the way."

I think Christians struggle with shoulding because we genuinely desire holiness. We want to be growing in Christ. We want to be maturing spiritually. We don't want to be stuck in old sinful patterns. But anytime we try to force ourselves into roles that Jesus never asked us to fill, we end up wrestling with ourselves rather than resting in him.

You belong to Jesus. So follow him. Worship him. Obey him. Repent from sin. Grow in him. Yes, do all those things, but never believe for a moment he's molding you into some cookie-cutter version of what a woman should be. As Jesus sanctifies you, he separates the real you from all the bogus expectations you place on yourself, the ones that make you a lesser version of you. As you become more like Christ, you are actually becoming more like the woman you were always designed to be. (And the woman *I* was always designed to be serves pizza to her houseguests. Mama doesn't serve no crumpets.)

5. Give Yourself Some Gold Stars

When I was a new mom, an older woman approached me at church and stuck a gold star sticker on my sweater. "I know the work you do at home goes unseen," she said. "Here's a gold star for a job well done."

The gesture was kind of cheesy, but I almost cried. It was like, *Someone sees me! Someone knows!* You're going to think I'm a little nuts, but I went home and made myself a chart (kindergarten style), stuck it on my fridge, and for a time, I began to award myself gold stars whenever I had minor successes as a mom. (Changed a diaper today? Gold star! Put a bra on today? Gold star!)

No matter what season of life we're in, it's so easy for women to be self-critical, to list all of the ways we mess up. Shame robs us of self-esteem, and we forget we have gifts and talents to offer the world around us. We get stuck on all that we aren't—*I'm not a good enough Christian; I don't read my Bible enough; I'm not a grateful enough person*—and then our shame grows bigger still. When you're in the thick of shameful thoughts or living in the dark days of shame, finding moments to give yourself gold stars can be especially challenging. However, if you can find some little way to encourage yourself, that process can do wonders for your ongoing overcoming-shame work.

God has gifted you uniquely, and those gifts are worthy of gold star stickers. Obviously, you don't have to give yourself actual gold star stickers (although I hear all the cool kids are doing it). The idea is to find your own way of being kind to yourself and taking back some of the self-worth shame may have stolen.

6. Return to Jesus Again and Again and Again and Again and Again

The world is divided into two camps. The first, and, in my humble opinion, the greatest ever, is the camp filled with those of us who love Cadbury Creme Eggs, the Easter candy from heaven. The second camp is made up of those unthinkable others who, for some inexplicable reason, can't stand the candy egg deliciousness. (They probably hate children and bunnies too.) One devastating year, I bit into my beloved Creme Egg and discovered that, by some flaw of the manufacturing process, it was empty. No egg white. No yellow yolk. No gooey goodness. Just a sad little crumbling chocolate shell.

The effects of shame leave us like that empty shell, and sometimes we end up looking to anyone or anything to fill us. I've made a few snarky comments about old boyfriends in previous chapters, so to be fair to them, I'll admit that I came to most of my former dating relationships with empty hands, begging those poor boys to satiate a hunger in me they couldn't possibly have filled. It was never their role to fix my broken shell, and it was unfair of me to expect that from any human being.

And my poor husband. When people ask Kevin if he's read this book, he replies, "Read it? I've lived it."

He's joking, of course, but there's some truth to that statement. No one more than Kevin (besides me) has had to bear the burden of the repercussions of my struggle with shame. No one else had to deal with my insecure questions in our first years of marriage: "Do you still love me? Do you still like me? Do you still adore me? Are you sure?"

He's been such a loving, faithful, godly, and gracious husband. (Remember, the guy willingly wore twinsie T-shirts with me on our honeymoon!) But even so, Kevin, with all his charms, does not have the capacity to fulfill my deepest longings for love.

The woman at the well (John 4) is a prime example of another woman who looked to men to fill her up. She had given herself to six husbands, but one fine day, her true Husband, Jesus, stood before her at the well. He had loved her before she ever knew him. He stayed when the others left. He knew the amount of hair on her head and had counted the number of shameful tears she had shed. He knew the real her, and he loved every bit. She responded to the love of Jesus that day by dropping her water jar at his feet—releasing her tight grip on the past, on the men, on her sin, and on her shame—and acknowledging that he had always been, and would always be, the only one who could fill her empty places. He restored her crumbling shell.

Perhaps you're running from one romantic relationship to the next, looking for affirmation, looking to feel complete. Maybe you're thirsting for approval from a pastor, teacher, parent, boss, or even a friend. Only Jesus, the Living Water, can fill you in such a way that you become satisfied and yet never grow tired of drinking deeply. Return to him again and again and again. He is standing before you saying, "My daughter, I see you—all of you. Nothing is hidden from me, and yet no sin or shame can ever change my love for you. I like you. I love you. I adore you. And I can fix your broken places."

So return to Jesus. Give yourself gold stars. Stop shoulding. Enjoy the little things. Remind yourself of God's truth. Continue to acknowledge shame. Sharpen your weapons and become a shame slayer, one who is consistently and victoriously overcoming her shame.

You can spend your whole life sitting next to a throne, wishing you were the princess. Or you can take your rightful place as a daughter of the King and live your adventure. Claim that throne (and decorate the thing with gold stars while you're at it).

DISCUSSION QUESTIONS

1. What does it mean to you that God is the Overcomer who constantly overcomes?

2. Which of the six tips is most helpful to you right now?

3. What is one of your go-to Bible verses when you need some encouragement against shame?

4. In what ways do you "should" on yourself? What unrealistic or difficult expectations do you place on yourself?

5. Name a few reasons you have for giving yourself some gold stars. What are some of your accomplishments, gifts, or abilities?

6. If you feel comfortable, share about a time you expected someone or something, other than Jesus, to fill you.

7. If Jesus were standing before you today, what would you love to hear him say?

PRAYER

God, you are my Overcomer, and I want to live a life that exemplifies you. When shame rears its ugly head, give me your strength to knock it down. When I bury myself in shame or put expectations on myself that you don't, or when I look to others to fill me, please help me to listen to your powerful voice. Remind me to return to you again and again. You are the only one who can fill me, and I praise you for that. Amen.

MARY

Overcoming the Shame of Disordered Eating

I was sixteen years old when I was diagnosed with anorexia. The next couple of years were a mess of doctors appointments, therapy sessions, hospitalizations, setbacks, and occasional victories. After a long-term stay at an eating disorder treatment center when I was seventeen, I finally found the strength to start down the road to recovery. I was ready to leave anorexia in the past.

Although I had tried several times to seek recovery, something always pulled me back into the darkness of my eating disorder. I'm not 100 percent sure what was different that time, but I believe it was a combination of wanting to get better, knowing what I needed to do to get better, and the willingness to keep fighting to get better.

When I began college the following year, I was dead set on becoming a dietician. But as my freshman year progressed, I realized I wasn't passionate about nutrition. I had convinced myself I wanted to be a dietician because some part of me knew that being constantly immersed in food, numbers, and exercise would enable me to hang on to a piece of my eating disorder. It was like a security blanket, making sure I never got too out of control with food or my body. It was a major milestone in my recovery when I was able to muster the courage to talk to people about my unhealthy attachment to my career goal. That's when I knew for certain I was ready to let go entirely of my eating disorder.

When I finally admitted that my eating disorder was fueling my desire to become a dietician, I realized that I could use my victory over anorexia to my advantage and to the advantage of others. Instead of studying to be a dietician, I earned my degree in counseling and now work at a private practice. I have a deep passion for walking people through the dark places in their lives so they know they aren't alone. I want to help them the way God has helped me.

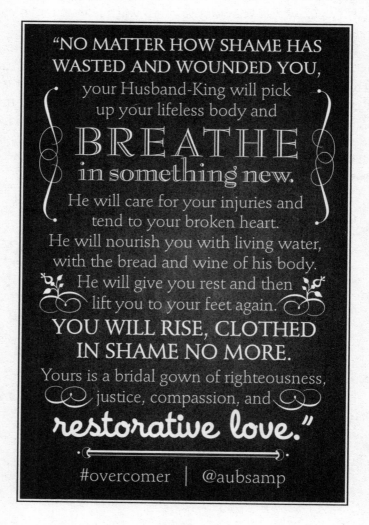

"NO MATTER HOW SHAME HAS WASTED AND WOUNDED YOU, your Husband-King will pick up your lifeless body and BREATHE in something new. He will care for your injuries and tend to your broken heart. He will nourish you with living water, with the bread and wine of his body. He will give you rest and then lift you to your feet again. YOU WILL RISE, CLOTHED IN SHAME NO MORE. Yours is a bridal gown of righteousness, justice, compassion, and restorative love."

#overcomer | @aubsamp

Chapter 9
GRAND OPENING

The Rest (As They Should Say) Is Herstory

A high school boyfriend once asked if I'd ever read the book of Hosea. I had. The words he said next still wreck me.

"You remind me of Gomer."

I sure knew how to pick 'em.

If you're familiar with the story, you know God instructed the prophet Hosea to marry an adulterous woman named Gomer. She had many lovers, but God instructed Hosea to continually love her, "though she is loved by another man and is an adulteress. Love her as the LORD loves the Israelites" (Hos. 3:1).

Hosea's marriage was to be an embodiment of God's relationship with Israel. A faithful and loving Lord had compassionately united himself with a people who repeatedly failed to honor their covenant relationship with him. They worshiped idols. They rejected their true Husband. They exposed themselves before other—lesser—lovers. Hosea and Gomer had three children together. Their first son was named Jezreel, after the site of a massacre (2 Kings 10). Their second child, a daughter, was Lo Ruhamah, meaning "not loved." Their third son was called Lo Ammi, "not my people."

Theirs is definitely not the kind of story you'd want illustrated in your children's Bibles. And Gomer is definitely not the person you want your boyfriend to think of when he looks at you.

—⟨⟨⟨✦⟩⟩⟩—

There is a little girl, an adolescent, a young woman who lingers in us. She longs to go back in time, to save herself from heartache, to rescue herself from pain. She is the daughter who played with princess paper dolls and dreamed of the day she would don her own tiara and white flowing bridal gown. She is the adolescent who had something stolen from her. She is the young woman hiding behind locked doors.

She once heard, and may have even believed, that Jesus died for her and could offer her the only way to eternal life. But she didn't understand that a full life with Jesus could begin now. She looked for fulfillment in so many other places, losing herself and remaining unseen, unfound.

We never set out to, but somehow we became that paper doll, flat and crumpled, a plaything with a need for repair and new clothing. We became empty and enveloped in the shadows of our shame.

Was I Gomer? Was I a daughter of Gomer?

You remind me of Gomer. Those hard words lingered in my heart for years. But God never abandoned Israel—or Gomer:

> "She decked herself with rings and jewelry, and went after her lovers, but me she forgot," declares the LORD.
>
> "Therefore I am now going to allure her; I will lead her into the wilderness and speak tenderly to her. There I will give her back her vineyards, and will make the Valley of Achor [trouble] a door of hope. There she will respond as in the days of her youth, as in the day she came up out of Egypt.
>
> "In that day," declares the LORD, "you will call me 'my husband'; you will no longer call me 'my master' . . . I will betroth you to me forever; I will betroth you in righteousness and justice, in love and compassion. I will betroth you in faithfulness, and you will acknowledge the LORD."
>
> —HOSEA 2:13–16, 19–20

This beautiful passage of Scripture teaches that even if you've given your heart away over and over again, even if you feel like that worn paper doll, even if you have been running from God, yes, even if you have betrayed the one who loves you, God will never abandon you. God doesn't leave you to rot in your mistakes. He doesn't punish you forever for your sins. He romances you. He draws you back to himself. He speaks tenderly to you. Where you had trouble, you will once again have hope. That which has been stolen will be replaced. Doors that have been locked will be thrown wide open. What shame has broken, he will restore.

No matter how shame has wasted and wounded you, your Husband-King will pick up your lifeless body and breathe in something new. He will care for your injuries and tend to your broken heart. He will nourish you with living water, with the bread and wine of his body. He will give you rest and then lift you to your feet again. You will rise, clothed in shame no more. Yours is a bridal gown of righteousness, justice, compassion, and restorative love.

God, who renews all things, eventually gave Gomer and Hosea's children new names. Their sons, once known for punishment and repudiation, he renamed "My People." Their only daughter, known as unloved, he gave the new name "My Loved One." Born into shame, loneliness, and misery, she was reborn as a woman deeply known and loved by her God.

And so it is with us.

You may have been Gomer.

You may have been a paper doll, used, marred, and tossed aside.

You may have been a shadow of yourself.

But in the name of Jesus, your Overcomer, your Shame Remover, you have been given a new name. Jesus says,

You are *Mine.*

You are *Loved.*

You are *New.*

You are *Radiant.*

Mapping Out the Path

Traveling the road from the girl whose boyfriend called her Gomer to a woman who is passionate about overcoming shame has been an adventure, to say the very least. In 2011, when I was pregnant with my third son, I took another step in that journey by applying for a mentorship program with author and speaker Shannon Ethridge. One of Shannon's books, as I have mentioned, played a significant role in my emotional healing, and I wanted to learn more from her. I was accepted to the program and flew down to Texas to spend time with her and a few fellow mentees. Shannon and I had a wonderful week together, hitting it off like sisters. At the end of my time with her, Shannon walked me through an exercise called Life Mapping.

Shannon invited me to draw a horizontal line—a timeline—across a sheet of paper. Above the line, I noted my most joyful and monumental memories from birth to the present. I wrote down my wedding day, the births of my children, and some other special events, such as the day I met Michael Jordan. (In case you're wondering, yes, he's very tall, and no, he did not invite me to play basketball with him. His loss, obviously.)

She then asked me to write my negative life experiences below the line. I jotted down the bus incident, my first breakup, the abuse I experienced at the hands of my boss, my grandfather's death, and a few other tender memories.

As I took in this bird's-eye view of my life, I recognized shame in a whole new way. I realized for the very first time how much the trajectory of my life had been driven by shame. I was able to identify a shame belief that first invaded my life that day on the bus: *I am special if I can attract the attention of the opposite sex.* That discovery helped me make sense of why, within just a few years of the bus incident, I allowed myself to return to my boss's office again and again. As much as I despised the experience, the toxic shame in me had me convinced his behavior was not only acceptable but desirable. Why? Because it made me special.

But shame wasn't the only thing I recognized in my timeline. In the middle of all of that darkness, I also saw the hidden hand of God. He had been there all along, protecting me from worse harm, opening doors of escape, and leading me into the life he so perfectly designed for me. He led me to a college nearly fifteen hours away. He brought kind and faithful friends into my life. He led me to my husband, a man who treated me with respect and kindness (and miracle of miracles, I was attracted to him). He gave me opportunities to encourage other women. He blessed me with three amazing and precocious boys. Even when I felt overwhelmed and lost in the midst of my shame, in my timeline, I could see a visual demonstration of God's love and redemption at work behind the scenes.

After that emotional exercise, I went for a long run in the Texas heat. (It's so hot there in the summer even your sweat sweats.) I love the benefits of running, but it is not a natural endeavor for me. I don't feel God's pleasure, or whatever that *Chariots of Fire* guy, Eric Liddell, says. I'm frankly a little skeptical that's even a true statement. I can usually manage to make it a few miles, however, if I'm distracted by podcasts or music. On this day, I chose to leave my devices at home in order to spend some uninterrupted time thanking God for his guiding hand over the course of my life.

As I dashed from one shady pecan tree to the next, I noticed how groupings of trees on either side of the road reached for the sky, creating a canopy effect above. Their leaves harbored me with shade and simultaneously gifted me with sunlit, sparkly patterns on the ground below. All at once, shadow and light were at play.

Overcoming shame is something like navigating that path beneath the canopy. The road may be unclear, murky, and dark at times. The effort may feel brutal and exhausting. In the end, though, we find that God guides us with tender grace and even dares to delight us along the way—a sprinkling of light on our dark path, rays from a resplendent sun cutting through the shadows, radiance in the midst of shame.

What Would You Say to Yourself?

When I mentor women, I often ask, "If you could go back in time and speak to the most ashamed version of yourself, what would you say?" It's a question I've pondered quite a bit myself. Here are the top ten things I would tell the younger version of myself, that girl behind locked doors.

1. Wear a tiara to prom. Who cares what people think? Who cares what the trends are? Wear a tiara because it's awesome—and so are you.

2. One day, you'll look back at photos of your first heartbreakers, the ones you spent days and months pining over. Believe it or not, you'll discover that they no longer have permission to speak into your life. You'll also discover that it's a good thing that's over. You can let go of it. It's okay to grieve and cry. But move on. Don't leave your identity there with the heartbreakers.

3. Be brave. I mean go for it! Do you want to travel? Do it. If the teacher asks if you want the lead in the school play, take it. Get friends together to start something.

4. Seek justice for and show compassion to those who can't speak up for themselves.

5. Begin a life of physical health now because you'll feel strong and rested if you jog or take an exercise class. But don't get obsessed. Exercise for the sake of the health benefits and the enjoyment of it.

6. You do not need to give your body away to prove that you are worthy of love. You are worthy of love because you were made by God, who is love. The body he gave you is sacred and valuable. It is not a cheap or

momentary thing for someone to use and discard. It is designed to be nurtured and cared for. Anyone who says or does otherwise is not worth your time.

7. You are not fat. You are not fat. You are not fat. You are not fat. You and your girlfriends will be tempted to look in the mirror and tear apart everything from your arms, legs, toes, and waist size to your hair color— even your gums. Step away. Don't give even a corner of your mind to such thoughts. You are only adding to the madness of a misguided, beauty-crazed culture. Instead, look in the mirror and say, "I am just how God created me—and it is good." Those words are worth shouting from the rooftops and whispering into ears. The I-am-not-enough lie is loud, but your voice and God's truth are louder.

8. Discover what you love and want to be in life, and work hard for it. No magic fairy will drop things in your lap. If you want to do something, find women you admire and ask them to mentor you. But don't rush. Through life's experiences, God will help you to discover who you are and what you are called to do.

9. Listen to your mother when she reminds you, "One of the old hymns says, 'Count your blessings. Name them one by one. See what God has done.'" That's not always easy, but it is a discipline that will lead you to a life of celebration. Thankfulness will remind you how good God is and how good you have it, even in the midst of hard times.

10. You will face some ugly and awful moments. Please remember, precious girl, that God turns ashes into beauty. He will turn the darkness into something remarkable and life-giving. I promise. Now, go get that tiara!

Cutting the Ribbon on Your New Home

Constructing the Overcoming Shame Identity is not easy. It's not built upon a perfectly manicured plot of green grass with a picturesque white picket fence around it. It's more like a monument rising from pain and difficulty. It once was war-torn and weathered but has been rehabbed into a marvel, a world wonder. And it is made more spectacular because of its difficult history. It is a lighthouse, brightening up the darkest night.

Thank you so much for going on this deconstruction journey with me. It's been quite a project. We've demolished the Shame Identity's lies and rebuilt an Overcoming Shame Identity on the truths we've explored throughout this book, truths all based on the ultimate truth: *In Jesus, I can overcome.* We've also read stories from some incredibly courageous women whose vulnerability and bravery I am so thankful for. I think the best way to honor them and to paint a fuller picture of the Overcoming Shame Identity is to give you a kind of Where Are They Now? update. (I love when they do that at the end of biopics, don't you?)

Catherine is overcoming shame.

Catherine, who wrote about overcoming shame from her childhood, shares this: "The hope and joy and faith I carry on this side of shame are incomparably stronger than what I lost. So much of what is good and strong in me are qualities Christ developed during my journey from shame to exile to redemption. I still sometimes *feel* shame, but I no longer *have* shame."

Zanna is overcoming shame.

Zanna, who wrote about the pressure she felt to have a perfect appearance, writes, "These days, instead of placing confidence in my clothes, I walk in the confidence of God. The reflection I see in the mirror truly is that of a woman made in the image of God. Instead of waking up in a silent panic, like I used to, I wake with a heart full of gratitude for the person God has created me to be. I glorify God with the words of the psalmist: 'I praise you, for I am fearfully and wonderfully

In Jesus,
I can overcome.

I am created in God's image with
exceeding worth.

God is able to evict
shame from my life.

God helps me release
the shame in my past.

With the help of my
community, I can
courageously overcome.

God transforms my shame
into radiance and
my misery into ministry.

Shame is in the mundane—
and there is a bright side to it.

True victory from shame is in the
willingness to continue fighting against it.

"Those who look to him are radiant; their faces
are never covered with shame" (Ps. 34:5).

made. Wonderful are your works; my soul knows it very well'
(Ps. 139:14 ESV)."

Diana is overcoming shame.

Diana, who wrote about the shame she felt when the older
men at church flirted with her, says, "I've come to realize that
shame is a consequence of sin. When I take my shame before
the throne of God, he looks down on me with love and releases the shackles that bind me. I no longer have to wonder what
I did wrong when someone wrongs me. Instead, I stand in the
confidence of knowing that God isn't the giver of shame; he's
the taker."

Rachel is overcoming shame.

Rachel, who opened up about the shame she experienced at
the hands of her father, writes, "Six months after I let God step
in, I graduated from college and started working as an addictions counselor. Every day at work, I am reminded of what God
has rescued me from. He has given me the strength and blessing
to work in darkness, acting as a light in this broken world."

Callie is overcoming shame.

Callie, who opened up about the shame of her unexpected
pregnancy, writes, "When I look back, I am amazed. Can it
truly be that this situation that once enslaved me in shame
has truly brought me such deep joy? We are living in the light.
We are free to enjoy our precious son and enjoy relationships
within our community without hiding and feeling ashamed.
We've chosen to live in grace, instead of living in shame. Fullest joy is ours. It is waiting for you."

Amy B. is overcoming shame.

Amy B., who shared courageously about her abusive marriage, writes, "Seven years after my divorce, I met and married a widower and adopted his two daughters. God indeed
puts lonely people in families. In this season of my life, shame
sometimes still whispers accusations: *You aren't a good enough
wife, a good enough mother.* It's never easy. But the road I've traveled has equipped me to distinguish lies from truth."

Amy N. is overcoming shame.

Amy N., who wrote about the high expectations she places on herself and the resulting shame, shares, "I no longer feel the shame I used to when I face difficult moments like the late-night crying session with Amber. I am in no way a good enough friend. I know that I never have been and I never will be. That's okay, though, because I know God is. He thinks I'm enough even when I can't live up to my own standards."

Mary is overcoming shame.

Mary, who wrote about her battle with anorexia, says, "Now I work as a counselor at an eating disorder recovery clinic, and my goal is to pay it forward—to share with others the life-changing care that I received when I was struggling with anorexia. I praise God that I'm here."

These brave women have taken up residence in their own Overcoming Shame Identity. Can you imagine what your life might be like if you did the same? What might your overcoming shame story be?

—❦—

My youngest son loves our family record player. His favorite albums are the seven inchers—the 45s—because each side contains only one song. Over and over, he says, "Mommy, turn the record over. Play a new song."

When Jesus releases you from shame, he turns the record over and writes a new song in and through you. He carefully deconstructs and then tenderly transforms your identity, so that you are no longer the person you once were. You are a new creation: an overcomer.

You may have been naked and ashamed, but in Jesus, you are clothed in courage, confidence, and dignity. You never again have to stoop in shame, because he is the lifter of your head.

You will never remind him of Gomer.

DISCUSSION QUESTIONS

1. When Jesus takes our shame, he offers us a new name: Mine, Loved, New, Radiant. What words or phrases come to mind when you imagine yourself with a new Overcoming Shame Identity? What would you like your new name in Christ to be?

2. As you think back over your life, the good and the bad, what themes stand out? How has God been at work in your life over the years?

3. Look at the image of the Overcoming Shame House. Which of the truths speak most powerfully to you? Why do you think that is? Which truths do you hope to begin growing in?

4. When you read the descriptions from the women who have shared their overcoming shame stories, which did you most relate to and why?

5. If you set a goal for yourself when you began reading this book, what was it? Share some of the ways God has helped you to achieve it as you've read these chapters.

6. What have been your biggest take-home messages from this book?

MY PRAYER FOR YOU

God, it's my turn to pray over the amazing woman who has just read this book. I praise you for how you've created her—uniquely, beautifully, a one-of-a-kind wonder. I ask that you bring her utter and complete healing from shame. Please set her free by your power, mercy, and love. Bind the evil one, and protect her from harm. Help her to rise in beauty from her ashes and to know without any doubt who she is in you and who you are in her. She is your beloved. She is your righteousness. She is your daughter. Give her the grace and strength to walk in freedom each day. When shame creeps in, help her to fight it boldly, knowing she is under the protection of your victorious banner. Glorify yourself in powerful ways through this woman's life. Help her to live as a woman unashamed, in you, her Overcomer. Jesus, I am so thankful for your power, your goodness, and your love. Amen.

YOUR STORY
Overcoming Shame

I know God is writing a powerful overcoming shame story in you, and I want to share it with others. If you've learned anything from God about overcoming shame and would like your story to be considered for publication on my website, *www.aubreysampson.com*, you can email me your story (in eight hundred words or less) to *yourovercomingshamestory@gmail.com*. By sharing your story, you not only take a step out of the shadows of your own shame; you also encourage every woman who reads your story to live without shame as well.

May you live shamelessly,

Aubrey

ACKNOWLEDGMENTS

A huge thanks, first and foremost, to my Kevin. Kevin, you have made many sacrifices so that I could be away from our life in order to stare obsessively at a computer screen. Thank you for always telling me to do whatever it takes to write. I love you. I like you. I adore you. You are a hunka hunka burnin' love.

And to my boys—you are my best blessings. You are my gifts from God. I can't wait to see the men you become and to meet the future women you'll treat (I know) with the utmost respect. (You better, 'cause Mama's watching you.)

Thank you to Catherine McNiel—the godmother of this book—for reading these pages more times than I can count and for making gentle suggestions over coffee and kids' squeals.

Thank you to my actual goddaughter, Amelia, and her fabulous mom, Gloria. And to my beautiful niece, Rose. You are in these pages.

Thanks, of course, to Redbud Writers Guild, without whom this book would not exist.

A massive thanks to the fabulous Shannon Ethridge for writing such a beautiful foreword amid a busy ministry schedule and for being a writing and speaking mentor, as well as a friend.

To Heidi Mitchell, my incredible agent at D. C. Jacobson—many thanks for seeing this book and believing in it from the start.

To Carolyn McCready, your investment in me as a communicator is invaluable. I appreciate you so much.

To Londa Alderink, Brian Phipps, and the amazing team at Zondervan—thank you for everything. I owe you a lot of coffee.

Thanks to my parents and my in-laws for their support. Thanks especially to my mom for flying in at several "last" moments to help me finish strong, and to my mother-in-law, Pam, for the hours of babysitting and prayer. I'm proud to call the Travises and the Sampsons my family.

Thanks to my sisters, Paige, Staci, and Corey, for making me laugh always and for your "beautiful depravity."

Thanks to Memaw, 'cause I just love ya! That breakfast at Cracker Barrel is among my favorite days.

To Brooke and Aubrey Pawlak, Ashley Egler, Katie Roper, and Amy and Katie Nickerson—thank you for caring for my boys while I hid away in a cave.

And, of course, to ma' girls—Jenn Ohlinger, Kathy Jack, Hollie Smith, and Amanda Weber—thank you for being shameless women. What would I do without you? And to Libby Tyner, Andrea Wickman, Mandy Apple, Kelly Wood, Tara Nichols, and Megan Kwacz—at various stages and seasons, each of you was a powerful lifeline. You are golden.

A special thanks to the Parnells and to Sheena—I wrote as I grieved, and thoughts of you were never far. Every field I see— airfield, bluebonnet field, baseball field—makes me think of Cam and that grin. Hook 'em.

Lastly, to the amazing women who shared their stories in this book—you are my heroes, truly.

NOTES

1. "What Is Sexual Assault?" Office on Violence against Women, US Department of Justice, July 23, 2014, *http://www.ovw.usdoj.gov/sexassault.htm.*

2. Brené Brown, *I Thought It Was Just Me (but it isn't): Making the Journey from "What Will People Think?" to "I Am Enough"* (New York: Gotham Books, 2007), xiii–xiv.

3. "Shame," Online Etymology Dictionary, July 3, 2014, *http://www.etymonline.com/index.php?allowed_in_frame=0&search=shame&searchmode=none.*

4. John Bradshaw, *Healing the Shame That Binds You*, rev. ed. (Deerfield Beach, Fla.: Health Communications, 2005), xxvii.

5. Mindy Kaling, *Is Everyone Hanging Out without Me? (And Other Concerns)* (New York: Crown Publishing Group, 2011), 7.

6. Beth Moore, *So Long, Insecurity: You've Been a Bad Friend to Us* (Carol Stream, Ill.: Tyndale, 2010), 92.

7. Jenna Fischer is credited with saying, "Let me please stand in solidarity with all of the women who are not a size 2 six weeks after leaving the hospital."

8. Brown, *I Thought It Was Just Me*, 95.

9. Amanda Weber in an email to the author, October 19, 2013.

10. C. S. Lewis, *The Weight of Glory and Other Addresses*, rev. and exp. ed. (New York: Macmillan, 1980), 16.

11. Brown, *I Thought It Was Just Me*, 95.

12. G. K. Beale, *A New Testament Biblical Theology: The Unfolding of the Old Testament in the New* (Grand Rapids: Baker Academic, 2011), 30.

13. "The Perfect Body," *www.dearkates.com*, October 31, 2014, *http://www.dearkates.com/blogs/diary/15637197-the-perfect-body*.

14. Shannon Ethridge, *Every Woman's Battle* (Colorado Springs: WaterBrook Press, 2003), 135.

15. Beth Moore, *Living Free* (Nashville: Lifeway Press, 2001), 75–76.

16. Henri Nouwen, *Seeds of Hope: A Henri Nouwen Reader*, ed. Robert Durback (New York: Bantam Books, 1989), 129.

17. Tom Wright, *John for Everyone, Part 1* (Louisville: Westminster John Knox, 2002), 22.

18. Cindy Johnson, *Who's Picking Me Up from the Airport?* (Grand Rapids: Zondervan, 2015), 120.

19. Ibid., 121.

20. Some of this content first appeared in a feature article I wrote. Aubrey Sampson, "Shame," *Fullfill Digizine* (Spring/Summer 2014), 6–8, *http://issuu.com/fullfill/docs/fullfill_shame_final/1*.

21. Robert H. Thune and Will Walker, *The Gospel-Centered Life* (Greensboro, NC: New Growth Press, 2011), 55.

22. Frederick Buechner, *Wishful Thinking: A Seeker's ABC*, rev. and exp. (San Franciso: HarperSanFrancisco, 1993), 119.

23. Christine Caine, *Can I Have and Do It All, Please?* (Sydney: Equip and Empower Ministries, 2009), 56.

24. Amy Poehler, *Yes Please* (New York: Dey Street Books, 2014), 71.

25. John Amodeo, "How Shame Makes Us Allergic to Receiving," *Psych Central*, February 27, 2014, *http://psychcentral.com/blog/archives/2014/02/27/how-shame-can-make-you-allergic-to-receiving/*.